The Holy Spirit acts sovereignl
his church. Charles H. Spurg
homiletical power and gifts of pr
and Spurgeon-stewarded. In tne miasι οι puoiiι ιιuιιuiι,
personal suffering, theological opposition, personal-appearance
caricatures, denominational disappointment, and too-many-
things-to-do, the Spirit blessed his ministry abundantly and
persistently. Conversions and growth in godliness were abundant.
That he was maligned so consistently and from so many angles
means, in his mind, that all glory belonged to God for the spiritual
power constantly exhibited from his pulpit and in the multitude
of benevolences originating from his church. Spurgeon not only
found the blessing of the Holy Spirit but developed a robustly
orthodox and experiential theology of the Holy Spirt in the
context of his preaching. Tyler Smiley has produced a thorough
exposition of Spurgeon's theology of the Holy Spirit. This volume
will encourage the readers to look for doctrinal instruction in
preaching as a path to the transforming power of truth. Smiley
has plumbed the depths of Spurgeon's doctrine of the Spirit, set
it forth clearly in the multifaceted operations of the Spirit, and in
the process provides both education and encouragement.

TOM J. NETTLES
Senior Professor, The Southern Baptist Theological Seminary
Louisville, Kentucky

SPURGEON'S LEGACY

Spurgeon's Theology
of the Holy Spirit

ALL HAIL, THOU COMFORTER DIVINE

Tyler H. Smiley

SERIES EDITOR: GEOFFREY CHANG

MENTOR

Copyright © Tyler H. Smiley 2025

paperback ISBN 978-1-5271-1271-1
ebook ISBN 978-1-5271-1369-5

10 9 8 7 6 5 4 3 2 1

Published in 2025
in the Mentor Imprint
by
Christian Focus Publications Ltd,
Geanies House, Fearn, Ross-shire,
IV20 1TW, Great Britain.

www.christianfocus.com

Series: Spurgeon's Legacy

Cover design by
James Amour

Printed and bound by
Bell & Bain, Glasgow

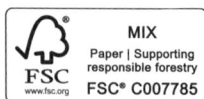

MIX
Paper | Supporting
responsible forestry
FSC
www.fsc.org   FSC® C007785

Dedication

To my wife, Catie, with all the love that I possess,
both now and forevermore

"All earthborn love must sleep in the grave,
To its native dust return;
What God hath kindled shall death outbrave
And in heav'n itself shall burn."

–CHS

The great King, Immortal, invisible, the Divine person, called the Holy Ghost, the Holy Spirit: it is he that quickens the soul, or else it would lie dead for ever; it is he that makes it tender, or else it would never feel; it is he that imparts efficacy to the Word preached, or else it could never reach further than the ear; it is he who breaks the heart, it is he who makes it whole: he, from first to last, is the great worker of Salvation in us, just as Jesus Christ was the author of Salvation for us. O soul, by this mayest thou know whether Salvation has come to thine house—art thou a partaker of the Holy Spirit? Come now, answer thou this question—hath he ever breathed on thee? Hath he ever breathed into thee? Canst thou say that thou hast been the subject of his supernatural influence? For, if not, remember except a man be born of the Spirit from above, he cannot see the kingdom of God.

—Charles H. Spurgeon, "Things that Accompany Salvation,"
The New Park Street Pulpit, vol. 3, sermon 152.
A Sermon Delivered on Sabbath Morning, September 20, 1857,
at the Music Hall, Royal Surrey Gardens.

1 The Holy Ghost is here,
Where saints in prayer agree,
As Jesu's parting gift He's near
Each pleading company.

2 Not far away is He,
To be by prayer brought nigh,
But here in present majesty
As in His courts on high.

3 He dwells within our soul,
An ever welcome Guest;
He reigns with absolute control,
As Monarch in the breast.

4 Our bodies are His shrine,
And He th' indwelling Lord;
All hail, thou Comforter divine,
Be evermore adored.

5 Obedient to Thy will,
We wait to feel Thy power,
O Lord of life, our hopes fulfil,
And bless this hallow'd hour.

—Charles H. Spurgeon, "The Holy Ghost is Here,"
Our Own Hymn-Book (London: Passmore and
Alabaster, 1866), 451.

Contents

Series Preface

Spurgeon's Legacy is a series of historical and theological studies related to the life of Charles Haddon Spurgeon (1834–1892). These volumes move beyond the existing scholarship of previous generations to engage with the latest research on Spurgeon's life and ministry within his Victorian context.

Spurgeon's Legacy will seek to cover a wide range of topics, including his doctrinal convictions, theological controversies, Christian spirituality, pastoral ministry, and philanthropic endeavors, all within the dynamic of his historical context. These topics will be explored from an evangelical perspective with appreciation for his contribution while being careful not to idealise the man or his ministry.

While seeking to be accurate historically, each volume will also have a practical and pastoral aim, bringing fresh insights and applications to church leaders and the broader church. By uncovering aspects of Spurgeon's teaching and ministry, these volumes will shed new light on contemporary issues and challenges facing Christians today.

Geoffrey Chang

Abbreviations

AARM – *An All-Round Ministry: Direction, Wisdom, and Encouragement for Preachers and Pastors.* Edinburgh: Banner of Truth Trust, 2018.

Autobiography – *Autobiography of Charles H. Spurgeon: Compiled from His Diary, Letters, and Records, by His Wife and His Private Secretary.* Volumes 1–4. Cincinnati: Curts & Jennings, 1898.

GFW – *The Greatest Fight in the World:* Conference Address. London: Passmore & Alabaster, 1892.

Hymnbook – *Our Own Hymn-book: A Collection of Psalms and Hymns for Public, Social, and Private Worship. London:* Passmore & Alabaster, 1866.

Lectures – *Lectures to My Students: Addresses Delivered to the Students of the Pastor's College.* Volumes 1–4. London: Passmore & Alabaster, 1881–1893.

Letters – *The Letters of Charles Haddon Spurgeon: Collected and Collated by His Son.* Edited by Charles Spurgeon. London: Marshall Brothers, 1923.

LS – *The Lost Sermons of C. H. Spurgeon.* Volumes 1–7. Edited by: Christian George, Jason Duesing, Geoffrey Chang, Phillip Ort. Nashville: B&H Academic, 2016–2022.

MSN – *My Sermon Notes: A Selection from Outlines of Discourses Delivered at the Metropolitan Tabernacle.* Volumes 1–4. New York: Fleming H. Revell Company, 1884.

MTP – *The Metropolitan Tabernacle Pulpit: Sermons Preached and Revised by C. H. Spurgeon.* Vols. 7–63. Pasadena, TX: Pilgrim Publications, 1970–2006.

NPSP – *The New Park Street Pulpit: Containing Sermons Preached and Revised by the Rev. C. H. Spurgeon, Minister of the Chapel.* Volumes 1–6. Pasadena, TX: Pilgrim Publications, 1975–1991.

Pictures – *John Ploughman's Pictures.* Philadelphia: Henry Altemus, 1896.

S&T – *The Sword and the Trowel; A Record of Combat with Sin & Labor for the Lord.* 37 Volumes. London: Passmore & Alabaster, 1865–1902.

TD – *The Treasury of David: Containing an Original Exposition of the Book of Psalms; A Collection of Illustrative Extracts from the Whole Range of Literature; A Series of Homiletical Hints Upon Almost Every Verse; And Lists of Writers Upon Each Psalm.* 7 Volumes. London: Passmore & Alabaster, 1869–1885.

Introduction
"Cradled in the Holy Ghost"

Charles Haddon Spurgeon (1834–1892) was the most well-known preacher of the nineteenth century, and his popularity in his time can hardly be quantified. On August 1, 1857, the Saturday edition of the *Dublin Evening Packet and Correspondent* simply stated, "Mr. Spurgeon is a notability."[1] Yet the article's most pressing question about Spurgeon's popularity was, "How is the matter to be explained?"[2] Spurgeon was only twenty-three years old at the time and had already led New Park Street Chapel to renovate and expand their facility to accommodate newcomers. During the renovation, the congregation moved their Sunday meetings to Exeter Hall, and to the congregation's amazement, crowds filled the temporary location to such capacity that the regular attenders were too numerous for the expanded Chapel.

The author of the 1857 newspaper article tried in vain to describe the reason for Spurgeon's meteoric rise in popularity:

> Mr. Spurgeon's origin and ecclesiastical connection do not solve the mystery.... We must add there is nothing in Mr. Spurgeon's presence to account for his success.... His figure is short and chubby, and rather awkward than otherwise. For so young a man there seems to be a strong tendency in him to grow stout. He knows nothing of the aesthetics of dress: everything of that sort about him is commonplace, verging upon the vulgar.[3]

---

1. "Charles Spurgeon and the Pulpit," *Dublin Evening Packet and Correspondent*, August 1, 1857, 3.
2. Ibid.
3. Ibid.

Crowds of "common people ... professional men, senatorial men, ministers of state, and peers of the realm," were flocking to hear this new and dynamic young preacher.[4] Still, something more than mere words drew the people; there was "something very extraordinary in [his words] everyone must feel."[5] His popularity was obvious and his influence was palpable, but the reason for his popularity was not easily explained.

Even more inexplicably, the August 1, 1857 *Dublin Evening Packet* article was published less than ten months after the Royal Surrey Music Hall disaster, which was caused by the actions of individuals intending to disrupt the growing influence of Spurgeon's ministry. On the Sunday evening service of October 19, 1856, during Spurgeon's pastoral prayer, some in the crowd falsely cried out that a fire was in the building, and caused a panic among the 12,000 in attendance. As people in the galleries evacuated in haste, some fell down a staircase and were trampled beneath the crowd. Seven persons lost their lives, and twenty-eight needed medical attention. In his final sermon at the New Park Street Chapel, before moving to the Metropolitan Tabernacle, Spurgeon reflected on that tragic event:

> I am sure that when we first went to the Surrey Music Hall, God went with us. Satan went too, but he fled before us. That frightful calamity, the impression of which can never be erased from my mind, turned out in the providence of God to be one of the most wonderful means of turning public attention to special services. And I do not doubt that it—fearful catastrophe though it was—has been the mother of multitudes of blessings. The Christian world noted the example, they saw its after-success, they followed it, and to this day, in the theater and in the cathedral, the Word of God is preached where it was never preached before.[6]

Nothing could stop or disrupt the growth of Spurgeon's ministry. Despite the devastating catastrophe, his utter unimpressiveness in appearance, his undignified social status, and the negativity he received in the press, his popularity only grew. In fact, requests

4. Ibid.
5. Ibid.
6. *MTP* 7.166.

for the young minister became so overwhelming that on Saturday, June 15, 1861, just thirteen weeks after the opening service of the Metropolitan Tabernacle, Spurgeon took out an advertisement in the *Salisbury and Winchester Journal* announcing, "Mr. Spurgeon begs to inform the public that he is knocked up with hard work, and is compelled to go into the country to rest. This will upset all his arrangements, and he begs his friends to remit his promises, and the Christian public not to inundate him with invitations."[7]

Spurgeon's notability persisted throughout his ministry. Over the course of his pastorate, crowds poured into the Metropolitan Tabernacle, and the reputation of his great preaching spread across the Atlantic at an unquenchable pace. In 1856, *The North American Review* evaluated the edited volume by E. L. Magoon titled *The Modern Whitefield: The Rev. C. H. Spurgeon, of London. His Sermons. With an Introduction and Sketch of His Life.*[8] The reviewer noted of the twenty-two-year-old Spurgeon, "His popularity is immense, exceeding that of any man since the days of Whitefield."[9] Two years later, the same journal again assessed Spurgeon with a disparaging review that mocked the preacher's sensibilities and reverence toward God, yet acknowledged:

> Besides these rapid issues from the press, [Spurgeon] has been kept prominently before us in the frequent notices of him transferred from the English journals, and in the letters of correspondents in England to our own journals. And we ask our friend who has happened to visit London, "Did you see the Queen?" and next, "Did you hear Spurgeon?" There is scarcely any name more familiar than his throughout our land.[10]

To hear Spurgeon preach was to experience Victorian London.

---

7. "Mr. Spurgeon," *Salisbury and Winchester Journal*, June 15, 1861, 7.

8. A. P. Peabody, "The Modern Whitefield: The Rev. C. H. Spurgeon, of London. His Sermons. With an Introduction and Sketch of His Life by E. L. Magoon," *The North American Review* 83, no. 173 (October 1856): 553–54.

9. Ibid., 553.

10. A. P. Peabody, "Sermons of the Rev. C. H. Spurgeon, of London, second series; Sermons of the Rev. C. H. Spurgeon, of London, third series; Fast-Day Service, Held at the Crystal Palace, Sydenham, on Wednesday, October 7th, 1857; The Saint and His Saviour, or the Progress of the Soul in the Knowledge of Jesus," *The North American Review* 86, no. 178 (January 1858): 275–80.

Throughout the years, friends and biographers also searched for the cause and empowerment of Spurgeon's ministry success. W. Y. Fullerton, student and friend of the great preacher, once asked William Robertson Nicoll, who also knew Spurgeon personally, "What then was the secret of [Spurgeon's] success?"[11] Fullerton explained, "He [Nicoll] must have asked it of himself, for without an instant's hesitation he answered: 'The Holy Ghost.'"[12] A friend of Charles and Susannah Spurgeon, W. Poole Balfern, once described, "[T]he secret of Mr. Spurgeon's success was, that he was *cradled in the Holy Ghost*."[13] Balfern's phrase stayed with Susannah for the rest of her life, and years later she saw fit to include it in Spurgeon's *Autobiography*. Likewise, in 1859, when Spurgeon's congregation broke ground at the future site of the Metropolitan Tabernacle, B. W. Carr presented a history of the church and its pastors. Describing the ministry of their present pastor, Carr pronounced, "So did the Holy Ghost accompany the preaching of the gospel with divine power, that almost every sermon proved the means of awakening and regeneration to some who were hitherto 'dead in trespasses and sins.'"[14] Years later, Iain Murray urged for the same in his biography of Spurgeon: "The true explanation of Spurgeon's ministry, then, is to be found in the person and power of the Holy Spirit."[15]

Spurgeon himself also credited the Holy Spirit for his ministry success. The person and work of the Spirit permeated Spurgeon's theology and teaching. His earliest sermon outlines, recently published as the *Lost Sermons*, provide glimpses into the young preacher's emphasis on the Holy Spirit. Spurgeon routinely made marginal notes in the hand-written outlines of these earliest sermons. He called these early outlines "skeletons," and on the illustrated title page of the first notebook from 1851 he wrote,

---

11. W. Y. Fullerton, *C. H. Spurgeon: A Biography* (London: Williams and Norgate, 1920), 317.

12. Ibid., 321.

13. *Autobiography* 2.181. All italics are original unless otherwise noted.

14. *NPSP* 5.350.

15. Iain H. Murray, *The Forgotten Spurgeon* (Edinburgh: Banner of Truth Trust, 2009), 38.

"Skeletons … and only skeletons without the Holy Ghost."[16] Likewise, at the end of sermon outline 143, Spurgeon wrote at the bottom, "Now I invoke the Holy Spirit."[17] Again, at the bottom of sermon outline 174 he wrote and twice underscored, "Holy Spirit, blow through me!"[18] In his earliest sermons Spurgeon relied on the person and work of the Holy Spirit for ministry fruitfulness.

Spurgeon's emphasis and reliance on the Holy Spirit continued throughout his ministry. In October 1851, he first preached at the church at Waterbeach where he subsequently served as pastor for more than two years. Two months after his first sermon at Waterbeach, the young preacher was preparing for the seventy-eighth sermon of his life when he penned a concise and Spirit-focused prayer that came to epitomise his pastoral ministry: "Oh Divine spirit give life, energy, fire and a blessing."[19] The Bible passage for that sermon was Matthew 11:28. Thirty years and six months later, Spurgeon again preached on Matthew 11:28 and modestly decried, "I wish that I knew how to preach. I have tried to do so for thirty years or so, but I am only now beginning to learn the art."[20] Like his seventy-eighth sermon, his sermon on June 12, 1881 was Christ-centred and Spirit-focused: "Oh, that one knew how to set forth Christ, so that men perceived his beauty, and fell in love with him at first sight. Oh, Spirit of God, make it so *now*."[21] Spurgeon, as it turns out, did know how to preach quite well, and he consistently emphasised the person and work of the Holy Spirit throughout his lifetime of ministry.

Spurgeon also exhorted other preachers to depend on the Holy Spirit in their own preaching. Later in his ministry, Spurgeon was pressed into producing his sermon outlines for publication. From 1884–1887 he published four volumes of sermon outlines on select biblical texts ranging from Genesis to Revelation. After the tremendous success of the first volume of *My Sermon Notes*,

---

16. *LS* 1.60.
17. *LS* 3.88.
18. *LS* 3.368.
19. *LS* 1.343.
20. *MTP* 28.650.
21. *MTP* 28.650.

Spurgeon rapidly produced a second volume in order to "lend a handful of chips and shavings, or, if you will, a bundle of firewood, to a brother, with which he may kindle a fire on his own hearth, and prepare food for his people."[22] As he considered the widespread use of the outlines, Spurgeon included a prayer of invocation in the preface: "May the Holy Spirit breathe upon these dry bones, and make them live! May he fill each preacher's heart with suitable emotions, and give to his mouth forcible expressions, and may the name of Jesus be thus made known to many of the Lord's redeemed!"[23]

The Development of Spurgeon's Pneumatology

But how did Spurgeon's theology of the Holy Spirit develop so early in his ministry? It is important to recognise that his theology of the Holy Spirit was not developed in isolation, but rather grew out of his interactions with theological writings spanning church history. The most profound influence on Spurgeon's theology came through his reading of Puritan theology. Ernest Bacon's biography, subtitled *Heir of the Puritans*, reflected the Puritan influence on Spurgeon's theology.[24] Even in his childhood years, Spurgeon spent days in his grandfather's library paging through volumes of Puritan works.[25] Later, when he described the gospel, Spurgeon would use a common refrain: the gospel came from Jesus Christ, was attested by the Scriptures, maintained by Augustine, Luther, and Calvin, and then passed through the Puritans. The final piece of the gospel heritage was always that it came through the Puritans. This was the theological tradition in which Spurgeon intended to stand.

Consequently, Spurgeon's emphasis on the Holy Spirit reflected the emphasis that existed among the Puritans. In the introduction to Abraham Kuyper's *The Work of the Holy Spirit*, B. B. Warfield argued, "[T]he developed doctrine of the work of

---

22. *MSN* 2.vi.

23. *MSN* 2.vii.

24. Ernest W. Bacon, *Spurgeon: Heir of the Puritans* (Grand Rapids: William B. Eerdmans Publishing Company, 1968).

25. *Autobiography* 1:22–24.

the Holy Spirit is an exclusively Reformation doctrine, and more particularly a Reformed doctrine, and more particularly still a Puritan doctrine."[26] In 1946, Geoffrey Nuttall likewise concluded that the doctrine of the Holy Spirit "received a more thorough and detailed consideration from the Puritans of the seventeenth-century England than it has received at any other time in Christian history."[27] J. I. Packer echoed the same sentiment a decade later in his paper "The Witness of the Spirit: The Puritan Teaching," where he noted/described that, "The work of the Holy Spirit is the field in which the Puritans' most valuable contributions to the church's theological heritage were made."[28] Michael Haykin, drawing on Warfield, helpfully summarised, "One of the distinctive marks of Puritan theology is its emphasis on the person and work of the Holy Spirit."[29] Spurgeon, then, was carrying on the theological emphasis that was handed down through the Puritans.

Like his Puritan forefathers, Spurgeon's theology of the Holy Spirit permeated his preaching, teaching, and pastoral ministries. The challenge of understanding, describing, and assessing Spurgeon's pneumatology is not due to a lack of material on the subject; rather, the challenge comes in that there is such a vast amount of relevant material. As Haykin rightly observed, "[S]o extensive is the material by Spurgeon on the person and work of the Spirit that it would take a monograph devoted to the subject to do real justice to his teaching on the Holy Spirit."[30] The fact that no such work has been produced sets this book as a needed addition to the field of Spurgeon scholarship.

26. In the introduction to Abraham Kuyper, *The Work of the Holy Spirit*, trans. Henri De Vries (New York: Funk & Wagnalls Company, 1900), xxxiii.

27. Geoffrey F. Nuttall, *The Holy Spirit in Puritan Faith and Experience* (Oxford: Basil Blackwell, 1946), viii. Nuttall argued, "Puritan discussion and interpretation of the doctrine [of the Holy Spirit] may be treated, indeed, as a vantage-ground from which to survey, and better to understand, the various contributions and emphases of the Puritan movement as a whole" (Ibid.).

28. J. I. Packer, ed., *Puritan Papers* (Phillipsburg, N.J: P&R Publishing, 2000), 17.

29. Michael A. G. Haykin, "'Where the Spirit of God Is, There Is Power': An Introduction to Spurgeon's Teaching on the Holy Spirit," *Churchman* 106, no. 3 (1992):198.

30. Ibid.

Outline of the Book

This book is divided into two main sections. Part I will consider Spurgeon's belief and teaching on the *nature* of the Holy Spirit; Part II will look at his teaching on the *work* of the Holy Spirit. Here is a brief description of the aim of each chapter:

Part I: *chapter 1* presents Spurgeon's Trinitarian theology, which grounded all of his theology and particularly his theology of the Holy Spirit; *chapter 2* presents Spurgeon's argument that the Holy Spirit is a person; and *chapter 3* provides Spurgeon's argument for the deity of the Holy Spirit.

Part II: *chapter 4* is Spurgeon's description of the Holy Spirit's role in inspiring Scripture; *chapter 5* addresses the Spirit's role in creation; *chapter 6* presents Spurgeon's understanding of the Spirit's role in relation to the incarnation, life, ministry, death, and resurrection of Jesus Christ; and the topic of *chapter 7* is Spurgeon's theology of the covenant of grace, and specifically the Spirit's role in the covenant.

Chapters 8–16, then, focus on the Holy Spirit's work directly toward the Christian and the church. *Chapter 8* details the Spirit's work in regeneration; *chapter 9* is on the Spirit's work in conversion; *chapter 10* is on the Spirit's work in sanctification; and *chapter 11* is on the Spirit's role in the perseverance of the Christian. *Chapter 12* introduces Spurgeon's understanding of the Holy Spirit's role within the church; *chapter 13* concentrates on the Spirit's role in the ordinances (i.e., baptism and the Lord's Supper); *chapter 14* presents Spurgeon's belief in the Spirit's role in preaching; *chapter 15* covers the Spirit's role in evangelism; and *chapter 16* investigates Spurgeon's descriptions of spiritual gifts, and how the Holy Spirit utilises those gifts in the church and in the world.

Part I

The Nature of the Holy Spirit

1

"Jehovah whom we Worship"
Trinitarian Theology

The doctrine of the Trinity is especially taught in Holy Scripture. The word certainly does not occur, but the three divine persons of the One God are frequently and constantly mentioned, and Holy Scripture is exceedingly careful that we should all receive and believe that great truth of the Christian religion, that the Father is God, that the Son is God, that the Spirit is God, and yet there are not three Gods but one God: though they be each of them very God of very God, yet three in one and one in three is the Jehovah whom we worship.[1]

In January 1856, Spurgeon completed the preface to the first edition of *The New Park Street Pulpit*. This initial collection included fifty-three sermons from the years 1855–1856, which were bound together as the first of what would become a sixty-three-volume set containing 3,544 sermons preached by Spurgeon. When Pilgrim Publications began republishing the sermon volumes in the 1960s they added illustrations at the beginning of each volume depicting Spurgeon's life and ministry. The frontispiece for the first volume included a picture of the young preacher standing in his favorite preaching pose—the index finger of his right hand pointed up toward the heavens. He was clean-shaven with brushed hair, slender, and his eyes were gazing upward and into the distance, as if he had seen something far off that he would make known. At the same location in the final

---

1. *NPSP* 4.289.

volume of sermons (volumes 62 and 63) there is another picture of Spurgeon. This time, the prince of preachers was sitting, right hand grasping a small book, and left foot propped on a small stool, no doubt to ease the swelling in his tired feet. In this later picture, he is bearded with wavy, dishevelled hair, and is now a rounded figure—the buttons on his vest were bulging. His face was still joyful, but in this picture his eyes were gazing downward, as if contemplating his lifetime of effort in ministry.

The juxtaposition of these two portraits contains the story of a man who dedicated himself to "the preaching of the Word."[2] Each subsequent volume in the set of sermons contained fresh sermons and new ministry updates, depicted in the illustrated images of the Pilgrim Publication set, tracing the life and ministry of the great preacher. So much changed about the man and his ministry as the years passed by. Even the title of the set changed after the first six volumes—following the relocation and renaming of the church— from the *New Park Street Pulpit* to the *Metropolitan Tabernacle Pulpit*. However, one constant remained unchanged throughout every volume of the collection of sermons from original publications—namely, the dedication page in all sixty-three volumes:

> To The One God Of Heaven And Earth
> In The Trinity Of His Sacred Persons,
> Be All Honour And Glory
> World Without End, Amen.
> To The Glorious Father, And The Covenant God Of Israel;
> To The Gracious Son, The Redeemer Of His People;
> To The Holy Ghost The Author Of Sanctification;
> Be Everlasting Praise For That Gospel Of The Free Grace Of God,
> Herein Proclaimed Unto Men.

Spurgeon's intention underlying all of his ministry was to proclaim and praise the "one God of heaven and earth in the Trinity of his sacred Persons." Spurgeon's theology was fundamentally, and steadfastly, Trinitarian.

---

2. *NPSP* 1.Preface.

Given the emphasis of the present work, this chapter will not seek to provide a co

mplete review of Spurgeon's Trinitarian theology.[3] Here, we will see that Spurgeon developed his pneumatology within a Trinitarian framework. He believed that Christian theology begins with a knowledge of the Triune God, and, therefore, the proper way to situate Spurgeon's theology of the Holy Spirit is by confirming his commitment to the historical doctrine of the Trinity.

Jehovah

When Spurgeon used the personal name for God, Jehovah, he understood it as a reference to the one God who exists eternally as Father, Son, and Holy Spirit. For Spurgeon, the name Jehovah, more than any other word or phrase, captured the reality of the one God eternally existing in three persons. In the first words of the first sermon in the first volume of the *New Park Street Pulpit,* Spurgeon proclaimed, "I believe … the proper study of a Christian is the Godhead. The highest science, the loftiest speculation, the mightiest philosophy, which can ever engage the attention of a child of God, is the name, the nature, the person, the work, the doings, and the existence of the great God whom he calls his Father."[4] In that sermon, he celebrated the greatness of God by considering "the immutability of the glorious Jehovah."[5] The name Jehovah indicated to Spurgeon that God "changes not *in His essence.*"[6] He admitted, "We cannot tell you what Godhead is. We do not know what substance that is which we call God. It is an existence, it is a being. But what that is we know not."[7] Nonetheless, it was that "marvelous incommunicable name—the name Jehovah," by which Spurgeon understood that "though He

---

3.   For a summative description of Spurgeon's Trinitarianism, see my chapter titled "Spurgeon's Doctrine of the Trinity" in the forthcoming book *Spurgeon in Context: History, Theology, and Ministry,* eds., Geoffrey Chang and Alex DiPrima (Brentwood: B&H Publishing Group, 2025).

4.   *NPSP* 1.1.

5.   *NPSP* 1.1.

6.   *NPSP* 1.2.

7.   *NPSP* 1.2.

is one God, we are taught in Scripture that He is one God in three most glorious persons."[8]

From two different sermons, twenty years apart, Spurgeon's affirmation of the Triune nature of God was clearly stated. First, in a September 1856 sermon, Spurgeon preached plainly, "Our God, then, is to be understood as Father, Son, Holy Ghost!"[9] Twenty years later, in a sermon in 1876, Spurgeon gave a biblical explanation of who this God is. He began with the Old Testament confession of Ruth to Naomi— "Thy God [shall be] my God" (Ruth 1:16)—and described that in her confession Ruth "had come to put her trust under the wings of Jehovah, the living God."[10] Spurgeon then asserted his belief that Jesus Christ is "very God of very God," and next celebrated the "action of the Spirit of God … the Holy Spirit" who accomplished regeneration "by the hand of God."[11] To be all the more clear on his belief in the deity of the Holy Spirit, in the sermon Spurgeon referred to him as "God the Holy Spirit."[12] If there remained any doubt as to the preacher's doctrine regarding the nature of God, Spurgeon summarised:

> Let us reflect upon … his nature, his person, his essence. There is Father, Son, and Holy Spirit — three in one: then the Father is my God: he hath loved me, he hath chosen me, he hath begotten me, hath provided for me, he is my Father, my all. Then, too, the adorable Son is mine — Jesus, the Redeemer, the Prophet, Priest, and King, the Intercessor, the Judge, is mine. Then the Holy Spirit is mine — the Instructor, the Quickener, the Sanctifier, the Comforter. Dew, fire, wind, dove — whatever the metaphor under which he veils himself — he is mine. The Father, the Son, the Holy Spirit — to these beloved and glorious of the one undivided Godhead faith says, "My God."[13]

---

8. *MTP* 7.153.

9. *MTP* 7.153.

10. *MTP* 22.314

11. *MTP* 22.320.

12. *MTP* 22.314.

13. *MTP* 22.321–322.

Creeds, Confession, and Catechism

Spurgeon's commitment to the historical doctrines of the Christian faith also highlighted his Trinitarian underpinnings. The creeds, confession, and catechisms that were especially relevant in revealing Spurgeon's Trinitarianism were, respectively: the Apostles' Creed, the Nicene Creed, and the Athanasian Creed; the 1689 London Baptist confession of faith; and, the *Shorter Catechism of the Westminster Assembly*, Keach's *Baptist Catechism*, and Spurgeon's own *A Puritan Catechism*.

Creeds

Throughout his ministry, Spurgeon commended the Apostles' Creed, the Nicene Creed, and the Athanasian Creed as true statements of faith.[14] At various times in his teaching ministry, Spurgeon acknowledged each of these creeds as exemplary. On one occasion, Spurgeon recounted a story of a German martyr who was tied to the stake making his final confession before the bundle of wood was set aflame. As Spurgeon explained, the man professed, "I freely admit that I am a poor sinner, but positively deny that I am a heretic, because from my heart I believe and confess all that is contained in the Apostles' Creed."[15] For Spurgeon, as for that martyr, the Apostles' Creed, which is explicitly Trinitarian, was evidence of a person's commitment to Christian orthodoxy. Likewise, in Spurgeon's sermon titled "A Gospel Promise," he reflected on the Athanasian Creed, "the soundness of whose teaching I do not question, for I believe it all."[16] And in the same way, he often commended the Nicene Creed as true and helpful in its description of Christian belief.[17] Spurgeon valued these creeds, which affirmed belief in the Triune God, as fundamental, concise, and true statements of the Christian faith.

---

14. References to the "Nicene Creed" indicate the statement that is more properly called the Niceno-Constantinopolitan Creed. This is consistent with Spurgeon's use of that title.

15. *NPSP* 4.117.

16. *MTP* 62.315.

17. See *MTP* 13, sermon 765; *MTP* 27, sermon 1631; *MTP* 40, sermon 2382; *MTP* 45, sermon 2635; and Spurgeon's remarks at the groundbreaking ceremony of the Metropolitan Tabernacle in *NPSP* 5, sermons 268–270.

More specifically, Spurgeon believed that these creeds developed the doctrinal nuances that assisted in properly understanding Trinitarian theology. Given the "many attempts made by the fathers of the Church to explain the relationship between the two Divine Persons, the Father and the Son," Spurgeon recognised:

> Suffice it for us to say that, in the most appropriate language of the Nicene Creed, Christ is "God of God, Light of Light, very God of very God." He is co-equal with the Father; though how that is, we know not. He stands in the nearest possible relationship to the Father,— a relationship of intense love and delight, so that the Father says of him, "This is my beloved Son." Yea, he is one with the Father, so that there is no separating them.[18]

Similarly, in the first sentence of his September 22, 1878 sermon, Spurgeon stated, "We do not find the doctrine of the Trinity in Unity set forth in Scripture in formal terms, such as those which are employed in the Athanasian creed."[19] While Spurgeon admitted that Trinitarian theology was difficult to comprehend, even as affirmed in the creeds, still he confessed, "We solemnly subscribe to the creed of St. Athanasius."[20] Capturing the heart of creeds, Spurgeon enjoined, "[T]hough there are not three Gods, but one God, yet there are three persons in the glorious Trinity in unity of the everlasting Jehovah, unto whom belong the shouts of the universe, the songs of angels, and the ascription of our united praise. Our God, then, is to be understood as Father, Son, Holy Ghost!"[21] Spurgeon believed that the creeds assisted the Christian by displaying right theology, which leads to true praise of God. Even so, Spurgeon knew it was the Spirit who opens the mind and heart of a person to recognise the truth about God found in the creeds. During his July 26, 1888 sermon, Spurgeon paused in the middle of his preaching to pray, "Blessed Spirit, abide with us,

---

18. *MTP* 45.386–387.

19. *MTP* 24.529.

20. *MTP* 7.153.

21. *MTP* 7.153.

take of the things of Christ, and show them to us, that so Christ may be glorified."[22]

As much as Spurgeon affirmed and utilised these creeds, he did not read them uncritically. He understood the creeds as true only insofar as they accurately represented Scripture, which is the Christian's ultimate authority. In his sermon on April 9, 1876, Spurgeon warned his congregation, "There is a fierce battle, still raging in the world, *between Scripture and tradition,*—between this Grand Old Book and certain things which have been handed down, by tradition, from the fathers."[23] Spurgeon was ever concerned with placing too much authority in historical statements of faith. He asked a series of rhetorical questions, "Well, dear friends, are you on the side of God's Word or of man's word? Is your rule of life, 'Thus saith the Lord,' or 'Thus say the fathers,' or 'Thus say the councils,' or 'Thus say the popes?' Who is on the Lord's side in this matter?"[24] Finally, the preacher decried:

> At this moment, I have not an atom of respect for any authority, in matters relating to divine truth, except the authority of God; and I would strongly urge all young people to try all catechisms, creeds, customs, doctrines, practices, and everything else, by that infallible test … "if they speak not according to this word, it is because there is no light in them."[25]

Even with his commendation of the historical creeds, Spurgeon was careful to identify Scripture as the Christian's sole authority.[26] With that qualification in place, Spurgeon gladly affirmed the Apostles' Creed, the Nicene Creed, and the Athanasian Creed as

---

22. *MTP* 40.488.

23. *MTP* 50.243.

24. *MTP* 50.243.

25. *MTP* 50.247.

26. Spurgeon's primary concern with the Athanasian Creed was the anathema included therein. He explained in a sermon, "I shrink with horror from the abominable anathema which assert that a man who hesitates to endorse [the creed] will 'without doubt perish everlastingly'" (*MTP*, 62.315). Preaching on John 20:31, he argued that the text "does not say, 'These are written that ye might believe the Athanasian creed' … No, no: 'These are written that ye might believe that Jesus is the Christ, the Son of God, and that believing ye might have life through his name'" (*MTP* 27.659–660). Again, he acknowledged, "No one may dare to say that a belief in the Athanasian creed will ensure us of salvation" (*MTP* 16.674).

true assessments of the Christian faith and helpful descriptions
of biblical teaching, particularly in regard to Trinitarian
theology. By affirming the truthfulness of these creeds, Spurgeon
situated himself within the historically orthodox and Trinitarian
Christian faith.

Confession

In addition to the creeds, Spurgeon also pointed to the 1689
London Confession of Faith as a trustworthy affirmation
of the Triune nature of God. In 1855, Spurgeon urged his
publishers, Passmore and Alabaster, to reprint an edition of the
1689 Confession. The reprinted edition was titled, *Thirty-Two
Articles of Christian Faith and Practice; or, Baptist Confession
of faith, with Scripture Proofs, Adopted by the Ministers and
Messengers of the General Assembly, Which Met in London in
1689, with a Preface by the Rev. C. H. Spurgeon.*[27] As with the
creeds, Spurgeon qualified that the Confession was "not issued
as an authoritative rule, or code of faith ... but as an assistance
to you in controversy, a confirmation in faith, and a means of
edification in righteousness."[28] This confession, then, was a useful
tool for explaining and understanding what the Scriptures taught.
Spurgeon described it as a "Body of Divinity in small compass
... to the Word of God, which is here mapped out to you."[29] With
this proper understanding in place, he commended, "This ancient
document is a most excellent epitome of the things most surely
believed among us."[30] As such, he included a copy of the 1689
Confession as one of the documents to be buried beneath the
foundation stone of the Metropolitan Tabernacle.

The 1689 Confession of Faith was inherently Trinitarian.
After establishing the sufficiency, infallibility, and authority of
Scripture, the second chapter of the Confession affirmed the

27. *Thirty-Two Articles of Christian Faith and Practice; or, Baptist Confession of faith, with Scripture Proofs, Adopted by the Ministers and Messengers of the General Assembly, Which Met in London in 1689, with a Preface by the Rev. C. H. Spurgeon,* 3rd ed. (London: Passmore & Alabaster, 1857).

28. *Autobiography* 2.160.

29. *Autobiography* 2.160–61.

30. *Autobiography* 2.160.

eternal Triune nature of God: "II.1. The Lord our God is but (a) one only living, and true God ... II.3. In this divine and infinite Being there are three subsistences, (d) the Father, the Word or Son, and Holy Spirit, of one substance, power, and eternity, each having the whole divine essence, (e) yet the essence undivided."[31] Spurgeon's hope for the 1855 Passmore and Alabaster edition of the Confession was to promote unity among Christians by clarifying the leading doctrines of the Christian gospel and promoting orthodox Trinitarian theology. Spurgeon provided two prefatory notes for this reprinted edition, one generally to all Christians and the other to his own congregation. To the general Christian population, Spurgeon urged, "I trust we are also kindred in spirit, and are striving together for the glory of our Three-one God."[32] To the congregation at New Park Street Chapel, he wrote, "By the preserving hand of the Triune Jehovah, we have been kept faithful to the great points of our glorious gospel, and we feel more resolved perpetually to abide by them."[33] In both notes, it was the Triune nature of God that Spurgeon headlined in order to promote unity in Christian doctrine. Just as Trinitarian theology was the bedrock of the 1689 London Confession, so too Spurgeon utilised this teaching as the bedrock of unity among Christians in his own day.

In addition to promoting Christian unity, Spurgeon also understood Trinitarian theology as practical for daily life. The 1689 Confession described, "[The] doctrine of the Trinity is the foundation of all our communion with God, and our comfortable dependence on him."[34] Reflecting on the preface he wrote for the 1855 edition, Spurgeon admonished later, "I would, at the present time, just as earnestly commend to my fellow-Christians the prayerful study of *The Baptist Confession of Faith* as I did in the

---

31. *A Confession of Faith, Put forth by the Elders and Brethren of Many Congregations of Christians (Baptized upon Profession of their Faith in London and the Country (1689)*, reprinted in *The Philadelphia Confession of Faith; Being the London Confession of 1689*, 6th edition, (Philadelphia: American Baptist Publication Society, 1907), 18–19.

32. *Autobiography* 2.160.

33. *Autobiography* 2.160.

34. *A Confession of Faith*, II.3, *Philadelphia Confession*, 20.

early years of my ministry in London, for I believe it would greatly
tend to the strengthening of their faith."[35] Spurgeon's ministry
was built on the Trinitarian theology that was fundamental to the
1689 London Confession of Faith.

Catechism

Finally, Spurgeon employed his own catechism as a teaching
tool to assist his congregation in understanding how Trinitarian
theology conceptualises the witness of Scripture. Following
the original version of the 1689 Confession of Faith, Benjamin
Keach, whom Spurgeon referred to as "my eminent predecessor,"
published *The Baptist Catechism* as a companion volume to the
Confession.[36] Keach was twenty-one years into his pastorate
when he produced his catechism for the congregation, which
then gathered at Goat's Yard Passage, Fair Street, Horselydown.
Spurgeon was only twenty-one years old when he published his
own catechism for that same congregation, which had come to
be relocated to New Park Street nearly one hundred and forty-
four years after Keach's catechism. As with Keach before him,
Spurgeon's *A Puritan Catechism* was intended as a companion
volume to the Confession of Faith. He explained, "I am persuaded
that the use of a good Catechism in all our families will be a great
safeguard against the increasing errors of the times."[37] If the goal
of the Confession was to produce a basic statement of faith to
guide the church, then the catechism was to make this theology
teachable in the homes of the congregants.

In creating his *A Puritan Catechism*, Spurgeon drew from the
Shorter Catechism of the Westminster Assembly and from Keach's
Baptist Catechism. Following with the Westminster catechism,
questions four, five, and six of Spurgeon's manual described
the nature of God. Question five asked, "Are there more Gods
than one?" and answered, "There is but one only (Deuteronomy
6:4) the living and true God (Jeremiah 10:10)."[38] Then, question

35. *Autobiography* 2.161.

36. *MTP* 50.601.

37. Spurgeon, *A Puritan Catechism with Proofs* (Albany, OR: Ages Library, 1996), 3.

38. Spurgeon, *Catechism*, 8.

six followed, "Q. How many persons are there in the Godhead? A. There are three persons in the Godhead, the Father, the Son, and the Holy Spirit, and these three are one God, the same in essence, equal in power and glory (1 John 5:7; Matthew 28:19)."[39] Spurgeon's theological starting point in *A Puritan Catechism* was the existence of God as Father, Son, and Holy Spirit. He understood Scripture to affirm that there is one God, that God is three persons, and that each person is fully God. While he knew that memorizing these answers would not equate to full comprehension of the nature of God, Spurgeon's intent was that "the words should be carefully learned by heart, for they will be understood better as years pass."[40] The creation and use of his own catechism showed that belief in the Triune God was the foundation of Spurgeon's theology.

The Inseparable Operations of the Triune God

Gregory of Nazianzus once explained, "[W]hen I say God, I mean Father, Son, and Holy Ghost."[41] The same could be said of Spurgeon. In a sermon entitled "My God," Spurgeon described, "To whomsoever Jehovah may be a name, he is God to me, and, as Father, Son, and Spirit, three persons in one blessed unity, I adore him."[42] Later, Spurgeon again praised "Jehovah, the one only living and true God," who exists as "three persons, all included, indeed, in the word Jehovah."[43] When Spurgeon spoke of God, he was speaking of the one who is Father, Son, and Holy Spirit. Equally, when he spoke of any one of the divine persons, he knew he was speaking of the one true God. Just as each divine person is inseparably one in nature, so too Spurgeon believed the works of the Father, Son, or Holy Spirit are inseparably one. This recognition and affirmation of God's inseparable operations, was,

---

39.   Spurgeon, *Catechism*, 8.

40.   Spurgeon, *Catechism*, 3.

41.   Gregory of Nazianzus, *Oration 38: On the Theophany, or Birthday of Christ*, eds. Philip Schaff and Henry Wace, A Select Library of Nicene and Post Nicene Fathers of the Christian Church, 28 vols. (Grand Rapids: Christian Classics Ethereal Library, 2016), 2.7.692.

42.   *MTP* 22.319.

43.   *MTP* 40.457; *NPSP* 3.399.

for Spurgeon, necessary in order to maintain sound Trinitarian theology, and was also particularly relevant to his theology of the Holy Spirit.

Even as Spurgeon followed the teaching of Scripture to assign particular works to the Holy Spirit, underlying his theology was a commitment to the indivisibility of God's work. This commitment meant that when Spurgeon taught about the work of the Spirit, he also understood each work to be accomplished in unity by the Father and the Son. The clearest examples of Spurgeon affirming the work of the Spirit while maintaining the indivisibility of God's operations are in his descriptions of creation, the resurrection of Jesus, sanctification, and the covenant of grace.[44] These particular examples are not treated by Spurgeon as isolated instances of Trinitarian operations, but rather they are clear and paradigmatic models for how God works.

Consider, for instance, Spurgeon's description of the resurrection of Jesus Christ. When Spurgeon taught on the resurrection he recognised that in various places in the New Testament the resurrection of Jesus was sometimes attributed to the Father, sometimes attributed to the Son, and sometimes attributed to the Holy Spirit. As Spurgeon explained, Jesus "was raised by the Father because ... he gave an official message which delivered Jesus from the grave. He was raised by his own majesty and power because he had a right to come out ... But, he was raised by the Spirit as to that energy which his mortal frame received."[45] This was not, for Spurgeon, a contradiction of ideas or a collection of smaller operations that added together to accomplish the resurrection. Rather, these individual attributions were an indication of how God works inseparably as Father, Son, and Holy Spirit in order to accomplish each and every operation according to his divine will. While a full review of this topic is not possible in the present volume, it is essential to recognise that Spurgeon affirmed the inseparability of God's operations

---

44. See chapters 5, 6, 7, and 10, respectively, in the present book. See also my chapter "Spurgeon's Doctrine of the Trinity" in Chang and DiPrima, eds., *Spurgeon in Context.*

45. *NPSP* 1.231.

while maintaining that the Holy Spirit, according to the biblical testimony, was the efficacious agent of God. Every action that Spurgeon attributed as a work of the Holy Spirit was grounded in his belief in the indivisibility of the nature and works of the Triune God.

Conclusion

In 1859, Spurgeon led his congregation through the groundbreaking ceremonies at the future site of the Metropolitan Tabernacle. As they laid the cornerstone for the physical structure, Spurgeon was intentional with each part of the service to show the theological foundation of the church. Just as the foundation stone represented the first block of the building, so under the stone Spurgeon buried a Bible, representing the true foundation upon which the church was built.[46] Tellingly, the services commemorating the occasion were richly Trinitarian. Spurgeon's opening prayer was offered to the "Lord, God" whose "throne is in heaven," and ended by praising, "unto Father, Son, and Holy Spirit be glory, for ever! Amen."[47] In the address he gave following his prayer, Spurgeon upheld the Nicene Creed and the 1689 Baptist Confession of Faith as reliable witnesses to the Christian faith. Finally, at the conclusion of the groundbreaking evening service, Spurgeon led the congregation in singing the Doxology, which praised God who is Father, Son, and Holy Spirit. Spurgeon recognised that the doctrine of the Trinity set Christianity apart from every other world religion, and, as such, the first and last words of the groundbreaking event proclaimed the Triune nature of God.

---

46.   Along with the Bible, other articles placed under the cornerstone of the Metropolitan Tabernacle included the Baptist Confession of Faith, the declaration that was signed by the deacons of the church and read aloud at the ceremony, and a copy of John Rippon's published hymnal (*NPSP* 5.351).

47.   *NPSP* 5.345–346.

2

"Dove from Heaven"
Personhood of the Holy Spirit

We are so much accustomed to talk about the influence of the Holy Ghost, and his sacred operations and graces, that we are apt to forget that the Holy Spirit is truly and actually a person—that he is a subsistence—an existence; or as we Trinitarians usually say, one person in the essence of the Godhead.... The Holy Ghost ... came down like a dove *from heaven* to show that it is from heaven alone that he descendeth.[1]

Three exemplary sermons, spanning over thirty-four years, display Spurgeon's consistent and long-term defence of the personhood of the Holy Spirit. First, the language of his January 21, 1855 sermon, captured in the quotation at the heading of this chapter, was echoed, secondly, in his March 1867 sermon where he described the Holy Spirit as "a distinct subsistence in the sacred Trinity."[2] Then, in March of 1889, referring to John 14:17, Spurgeon again declared:

"Ye know him," says our Lord; and truly we know the Holy Ghost as to his personality. If the Holy Ghost were a mere influence, we should read, "Ye know *it.*" Let us always shun the mistake of calling the Holy Ghost "*it.*" *It* cannot do anything. *It* is a dead thing: the Holy Ghost is a living, blessed person, and I hope we can say that we know him as such.[3]

---

1. *NPSP* 1.25–26.
2. *MTP* 13.121.
3. *MTP* 35.138.

Even so, Spurgeon did not merely affirm the personality of the Holy Spirit, but he provided a biblical argument to support the assertion. The four key categories that defined his argument for the personhood of the Holy Spirit were present in his January 21, 1855 sermon where he argued that "it is self-evident, that wherever you find understanding, will, and power, you must also find an existence; it cannot be a mere attribute, it cannot be a metaphor, it cannot be a personified influence; but it must be a person."[4] To those three characteristic traits—namely, understanding, will, and power—he added later in the same sermon, "Certain feelings are ascribed to the Holy Ghost, which can only be understood upon the supposition that he is actually a person.... [I]t is said that the Holy Ghost can be grieved."[5] So, Spurgeon's primary defences of the personality of the Holy Spirit, exemplified in his January 21, 1855 sermon, were the Spirit's knowledge, will, personal power, and that the Spirit can be grieved.

The Holy Spirit as Teacher

In his defence of the Holy Spirit's personhood, Spurgeon highlighted the Spirit's understanding, which is displayed in the Spirit's role as teacher. Spurgeon's preaching year of 1855 at New Park Street Chapel had at its beginning and end an emphasis on the teaching ministry of the Holy Spirit. On January 21, 1855, he preached a sermon titled "The Personality of the Holy Ghost," and on December 16, 1855 he preached on "Heaven." In the earlier sermon, Spurgeon declared that "a power of knowledge is ascribed to the Holy Ghost."[6] Since Scripture attributes knowledge and understanding to the Holy Spirit, Spurgeon argued, "I believe every rational man will admit, that when anything is spoken of as having an understanding, it must be an existence—it must, in fact, be a person."[7] In the later sermon, Spurgeon described the church's time together as "a little of the teaching of God's gracious

---

4. *NPSP* 1.27.
5. *NPSP* 1.28.
6. *NPSP* 1.27.
7. *NPSP* 1.27.

Spirit, whereby he reveals unto us what heaven is."[8] Spurgeon explained that the Spirit revealed to the Christian one's own sinfulness and "teaches [the Christian] his righteousness in Christ Jesus."[9] In his December 16 sermon, Spurgeon admitted, "I love to talk of the Spirit's influence on man."[10] Indeed, his love for talking about the Holy Spirit's teaching resulted in a year bookended by an emphasis on the Spirit as teacher. Since teaching was a primary work of the Holy Spirit, and teaching is only possible for a personal being, therefore the Holy Spirit must be a person.

As much as Spurgeon utilised the Spirit's role in teaching to affirm the Spirit's personality, it is not as if he treated the topic with heartless rationality. Spurgeon believed that the Spirit's personhood was essential because a Christian is able to know the truth about God only if the Holy Spirit teaches it to him or her. In March of 1889 Spurgeon returned to the topic of the Spirit's knowledge, describing this knowledge as "the truth of God."[11] Spurgeon proclaimed that the Holy Spirit "is the teacher of truth, unalloyed truth, practical, divinely effective truth. He never teaches anything but the truth. If it comes from the Spirit of God, we may receive it from him without any hesitation."[12] Even as the Spirit "takes the things of Christ and shows them unto us," the truth he teaches is from Christ, for the Holy Spirit is the "very Spirit and soul of truth, the essence, the life and power of it."[13] Whatever the Spirit teaches is God's truth, and the Spirit is uniquely able to teach this truth to human beings. Spurgeon explained that the Holy Spirit "makes the truth itself, in its reality and substance, to enter the soul, and affect the heart. He is the teacher of truth, and he is himself the active power that makes truth to be truth to us in the assurance of our inmost souls."[14]

---

8.   *NPSP* 2.21.
9.   *NPSP* 2.21.
10.   *NPSP* 2.21.
11.   *MTP* 35.134.
12.   *MTP* 35.133.
13.   *MTP* 35.133.
14.   *MTP* 35.133.

Spurgeon further expressed that the knowledge the Spirit possesses is rooted in the trinitarian relations of the Godhead: "There is such an intimate union between the Holy Spirit, the Father, and the Son, that, to know the Holy Spirit, we must know the Son of God, and know the Father. If we know the Lord Jesus, we have the Spirit of God; for by no one else could the things of Christ be revealed to us."[15] Ultimately, the knowledge between the Spirit and the Christian was relational, and if relational then the Holy Spirit must be a person with whom a relationship is possible. Spurgeon celebrated, *Ye know not only his work, but himself. I may know the great achievements of an artist in marble, but I may not know the sculptor himself.... truly we know the Holy Ghost as to his personality."*[16] The Spirit's work as a teacher was, for Spurgeon, a sure sign of the Spirit's personhood, and a necessity in order for the Christian to know God.

The Will of the Spirit

There is an important discussion in the history of Trinitarian theology as to whether the three divine persons share in a single will, or whether a will ought to be understood as a proper characteristic of individual personhood. Evidenced by the language he utilised in his teaching, Spurgeon wrestled with the best way to describe the divine will of God and the Holy Spirit's freedom to operate according to this will. As we have seen above, Spurgeon maintained the historically orthodox position that God's external works are indivisible. Given the indivisibility of the nature of the Triune God, so are the operations of all three divine persons inseparable. As such, a reasonable outcome is that there must be only one divine will and not a separate will in each of the divine persons, for three separate wills implies the idea of three Gods. Spurgeon avoided this error by his full affirmation of the indivisibility of the nature and work of the Father, Son, and Holy Spirit.

Nevertheless, in an effort to ascribe to the Holy Spirit the freedom to work and operate as God, Spurgeon pushed the limits

15. *MTP* 35.135.
16. *MTP* 35.138.

of the orthodox language regarding the will of the Holy Spirit. John Owen, addressing the same topic, wrote,

> the will of God as to the peculiar actings of the Father in this matter is the will of the Father, and the will of God with regard to the peculiar actings of the Son is the will of the Son; not by a distinction of sundry wills, but by the distinct application of the same will unto its distinct acts in the persons of the Father and the Son.[17]

While Spurgeon does not specifically refer to this theological teaching of Owen, this is a helpful paradigm that seems to capture Spurgeon's understanding of the will of the Holy Spirit.

So, for example, in the fourth sermon published in the *New Park Street Pulpit*, Spurgeon quoted 1 Corinthians 12:11, and stated that "it is plain the Spirit has a will."[18] Spurgeon nuanced this reading to explain that the Holy Spirit "does not come from God simply at God's will, but he has a will of his own."[19] Even in that sermon, Spurgeon was careful not to pit one person of the Godhead against another, and so he stipulated that the Holy Spirit "has a will of his own, which is always in keeping with the will of the infinite Jehovah, but is, nevertheless, distinct and separate."[20] While this may seem as if Spurgeon is dividing out the will of God into three separate wills, it is important to recognise that Spurgeon was using the theme of the Holy Spirit's will primarily as an argument for the personhood of the Spirit, and not in a discussion of the Spirit's divine nature. This is precisely the argument he is building in his sermon on 1 Corinthians 12:11. Thus, Spurgeon summarised the sermon's main argument about the Holy Spirit in a phrase: "Therefore, I say he is a person."[21]

Spurgeon's description of the will of the Holy Spirit was developed from other biblical passages also. First, in Hebrews 2:3–4, the text described that the gifts of the Holy Spirit

---

17. William H. Goold, ed., *The Works of John Owen* (London: Johnstone and Hunter, 1850–1855), 19:88.

18. *NPSP* 1.27.

19. *NPSP* 1.27.

20. *NPSP* 1.27.

21. *NPSP* 1.27.

were distributed "according to his own will." This was a phrase that Spurgeon employed with regularity in his preaching. For example, in his April 19, 1868 sermon, he argued for the will of the Spirit based on the Spirit's nature as God. "Now consider who the Holy Spirit is," Spurgeon defined, "He is the blessed God himself—one person of the glorious Trinity in unity."[22] Consequently, the Holy Spirit "can work according to his own will."[23] Later in his ministry, Spurgeon illustrated the phrase with a metaphor from two Old Testament passages. While on holiday in Mentone in January of 1887, Spurgeon gave an address from Song of Solomon 4:16. He commended the practice of prayer, though denied that prayer meant commanding the Spirit to work, for such a task would be like trying to "raise the wind."[24] Spurgeon argued that "we can no more command the Holy Spirit than we can compel the wind to blow east or west," because the Holy Spirit is "that great Spirit who operates according to his own will."[25] Likewise, two months later, back at the Metropolitan Tabernacle and preaching on Micah 2:7, Spurgeon referred to some unnamed opponents "*who would altogether have silenced the Spirit. They would banish all spiritual teaching from the earth, that the voice of human wisdom might be uncontradicted.*"[26] The biblical truth from two months earlier was still on his mind: "Is he not the free Spirit who, like the wind, bloweth where he listeth?"[27]

Second, the biblical metaphor likening the Holy Spirit to the wind, found in John 3:8, was one that Spurgeon used often when discussing the Holy Spirit. In May 1877, Spurgeon preached a sermon on John 3:8 entitled "The Heavenly Wind," which he taught as an instructive metaphor for the freedom of the Holy Spirit. Just as the wind blows when, where, and how it pleases, Spurgeon illustrated, "So is it, only in a far higher and more emphatic sense, with the Holy Spirit, for he is most free and

---

22. *MTP* 14.234.
23. *MTP* 14.234.
24. *MTP* 33.38.
25. *MTP* 33.38.
26. *MTP* 33.146 (emphasis added).
27. *MTP* 33.146–147.

absolute … for the Holy Spirit, he is God himself, and absolutely free, and worketh according to his own will and pleasure."[28] For Spurgeon, this volition ascribed to the Holy Spirit identified the Spirit as a person of the Godhead.

The Personal Power of the Spirit

A third argument of Spurgeon for the personhood of the Holy Spirit was that the Spirit maintained personal power. Spurgeon ascribed to the Holy Spirit a power and ability reserved in Scripture for God. When Spurgeon preached on Romans 15:13, he explained that in this text "*power* is ascribed to the Holy Ghost, and power is a thing which can only be ascribed to an existence."[29] Five months later, two days before his twenty-first birthday, Spurgeon again preached on the Holy Spirit's power from Romans 15:13. In this latter sermon, Spurgeon's overarching argument was, "Power is the special and peculiar prerogative of God, and God alone."[30] Indeed, the biblical description of the Spirit's power was, for Spurgeon, a clear indication for both the deity and personhood of the Holy Spirit. Spurgeon summarised, "The Holy Spirit has power omnipotent, even the power of God."[31] Certainly, the Holy Spirit's power proved his divine nature. At the same time, the Spirit's use of this power demonstrated the Spirit's personality.

Again, this power exemplified by the Holy Spirit was not merely a rational argument for a right understanding of the Spirit's nature. Because the Spirit is in his nature God, then the work of the Spirit in the life of a Christian is God at work, and the fact that the Spirit is a person means that this work is the intentional effort of the third person of the Triune God on behalf of the Christian. For Spurgeon, the power of the Holy Spirit in the life of a Christian manifested in two primary ways: the outward and visible displays, and the inward and spiritual manifestations. As much as the outward signs of the Spirit's power moved

---

28. *MTP* 23.303–304.
29. *NPSP* 1.27 (emphasis added).
30. *NPSP* 1.229.
31. *NPSP* 1.232.

Spurgeon to praise, the inward work, which is felt rather than seen, proved to Spurgeon the personhood of the Spirit. Spurgeon described the hidden operation of the Spirit on the hearts, wills, and imaginations of human beings. Consequently, the only one with the power to change the intellect, volition, or affections of a human being was God himself, and the way God accomplished it was by the work of the Holy Spirit. These changes in the Christian are personal in nature and directed toward an intended end, requiring the work of a personal being. The intentionality of the Holy Spirit was highlighted by describing how only the Spirit has the power to make an incorrigible sinner "impetuous after the gospel."[32] After regenerating and converting the Christian, Spurgeon also described the Holy Spirit as the Christian's "bulwark" and that "all his omnipotence defends you.... [T]he power of the Spirit is our power; the power of the Spirit is our might."[33] Spurgeon believed that the Spirit's hidden work to bring a person to faith in Jesus Christ and sustain a Christian in the faith was clear evidence for the personhood of the Holy Spirit. Spurgeon recognised that the Holy Spirit operated with divine personal power, and by this power he ultimately accomplished the regeneration, conversion, sanctification, and perseverance of the Christian.

Grieving the Holy Spirit

Spurgeon's fourth key argument for the Spirit's personhood was the true possibility that the Holy Spirit could be grieved. Based on Acts 7:51 Spurgeon believed that the Holy Spirit could be resisted; based on Acts 5:9 he believed the Spirit could be tempted; and based on Isaiah 63:10 he believed the Spirit could be vexed. However, it was the "astounding fact" that the Holy Spirit could be grieved, that was most lamentable to Spurgeon.[34] He was distraught to think that the "heavenly dove may be disturbed; the celestial fire may be damped; the divine wind may be resisted;

---

32. *NPSP* 1.234.

33. *NPSP* 1.236.

34. *MTP* 13.121.

the blessed Paraclete may be treated with despite."[35] The biblical basis for Spurgeon's position was Ephesians 4:30. He preached two separate sermons on this verse, on October 9, 1859 and March 3, 1867, respectively. In both sermons, he expressed the personal work of the Spirit as teacher, comforter, and guide, and as one who assists, confirms, preserves, and loves. Spurgeon referred to the Spirit as "one person of the Trinity."[36] In the 1867 sermon, Spurgeon began, "It is a very clear proof of the personality of the Holy Spirit that he can be grieved."[37] Insofar as the Holy Spirit can be grieved, and since "we can only grieve a person," Spurgeon argued, "we see that he is a distinct subsistence in the sacred Trinity."[38] The fact that the Holy Spirit could be grieved was, to Spurgeon, a clear argument for the Spirit's personality.

The things that cause the Holy Spirit to be grieved are deplorable and lamentable actions, and the result of these is the loss of the Spirit's presence, the loss of Christian joy, and the loss of spiritual power. When the Christian grieves the Holy Spirit, he or she loses all usefulness for God's work on earth. Instead, the Christian must, "Let the will of the Spirit be your absolute law.... Do not willfully shut your eyes to an unpleasant duty.... Lean not to your own understanding; consider that the Holy Ghost alone can teach you."[39] For Spurgeon, the possibility of grieving the Holy Spirit was a proof of his personhood, and the protection against grieving the Spirit was to know him as a person who teaches and guides the Christian into right living.

While Spurgeon described the grief of the Holy Spirit as a feeling or emotion, he also attempted to maintain the doctrine of God's impassibility.[40] This was a doctrine that Spurgeon struggled

---

35.   *MTP* 13.122.

36.   *NPSP* 5.428.

37.   *MTP* 13.121.

38.   *MTP* 13.121.

39.   *MTP* 13.131–132.

40.   Matthew Warren argues in his dissertation that Spurgeon modifies the classical view of impassibility towards the latter part of his life. Matthew Warren, *"A Fit Theme for a Holy Song": A Critical Analysis of the Views of C. H. Spurgeon on the Immutability and Impassibility of God,* PhD Dissertation, Midwestern Baptist Theological Seminary, 2024.

to hold together with his reading of the biblical narrative. In his October 9, 1859 sermon at Royal Surrey Gardens, nearing the two-year anniversary of the Music Hall disaster, Spurgeon explained of Ephesians 4:30, "Of course, the language is to be understood as speaking after the manner of men. The Holy Spirit of God knoweth no passion or suffering, but nevertheless, his emotion is here described in human language as being that of grief."[41] As one who experienced grief himself, Spurgeon wrestled with what it meant that God could be grieved.

Nearly ten years after that October 9, 1859 sermon, Spurgeon preached another one on the parallel between Abraham's offering up of Isaac and Romans 8:32. In the midst of the sermon, Spurgeon became so moved by the theme that he requested, "Brethren, suffer me to pause and worship, for I fail to preach. I am abashed in the presence of such wondrous love. I cannot understand thee, O great God."[42] And in the midst of the sermon, Spurgeon wrestled with God:

> I know thou art not moved by passions, nor affected by grief as men are; therefore dare I not say that thou didst sorrow over the death of thy Son. But oh! I know that thou art not a God of stone, impassible, unmoved. Thou art God, and therefore we cannot conceive thee; but yet thou dost compare thyself to a father having compassion on a prodigal.[43]

Spurgeon questioned, "Do we err, then, if we think of thee as yearning over thy Wellbeloved when he was given up to the pangs of death?"[44] Spurgeon was confident in God's immutability. He believed biblically and existentially that God was constant in times of distress. However, he failed to resolve the tension in that sermon between God's constancy and ability to be grieved. Spurgeon admitted, "Forgive me if I transgress in so conceiving of thy heart of love, but surely it was a costly sacrifice which

---

41. *NPSP* 5.425–26.

42. *MTP* 15.258–59.

43. *MTP* 15.259.

44. *MTP* 15.259.

thou didst make, costly even to thee!"[45] Ultimately, Spurgeon maintained, "I will not speak of thee in this matter, O my God, for I cannot, but I will reverently think of thee, and wonder how thou couldst have looked so steadily through the long ages, and resolved so unwaveringly upon the mighty sacrifice, the immeasurable generosity of resigning thy dear Son to be slaughtered for us."[46]

Later in his ministry, Spurgeon preached another sermon on the Father's love. This 1882 sermon focused on the theme of the Father's divine motive for the love, gifts, benefits, and kindness he shows toward those who are his children through faith in Jesus Christ. The Bible verse he preached from was Psalm 103:13: "Like a father pitieth his children, so the Lord pitieth them that fear him." As before, he referred here again to the "axiom in theology that God has no griefs,—that he is 'without parts or passions.'"[47] Again he struggled to see the theological affirmation as compatible with the biblical witness, only this time his struggle had become more soured to the idea that this language in the Scripture did not actually reflect any feeling or attribute of God. Spurgeon was dissatisfied with the notion that this language provided mere human language that was uninstructive metaphor. He even went so far as to contend, "I dismiss therefore the theology of the schoolmen; I am quite satisfied with the divinity that I find in these Scriptures. Believe it then, dear friends, with all your hearts, that God has kindly feelings towards them that fear him, such as a father has towards his children."[48]

On the surface, that affirmation may be received as a denial of the doctrine of God's impassibility. And, perhaps, Spurgeon did want to reject a view of the doctrine that led someone to believe that God "may be passionless, and without emotion, or without anything that is akin to feeling" like the false "gods of the heathen."[49] He certainly wanted to reject any notion that

---

45.   *MTP* 15.259.
46.   *MTP* 15.259.
47.   *MTP* 28.157.
48.   *MTP* 28.158.
49.   *MTP* 28.158.

the Father's "heart is unaffected or callous to our suffering."[50] However, even in this sermon, Spurgeon again qualified his position by affirming God's complete foreknowledge of "the end as well as the beginning."[51] Similar to his earlier wrestling with this doctrine, Spurgeon again affirmed that God's affection for his children is a real motivation for his benevolent action toward them. More than anything, Spurgeon seemed to push against a shallow doctrine of God's impassibility that implied that God could not act with compassion, love, grace, or mercy. Spurgeon held that God did indeed act with these types of feelings, but also acted only according to his sovereign will. As a prime example, just as he had described in his earlier sermons Spurgeon again referred to one of the most difficult ideas of the biblical testimony to the Holy Spirit—that "if the Holy Spirit is 'vexed,' there must be something analogous to what we call emotion among ourselves in the acknowledged attributes of the Most High."[52]

It is clear that Spurgeon struggled with a desire to affirm God's impassibility, and at the same time make sense of the biblical witness of the motivations for God's actions. Nevertheless, in reference to his theology of the Holy Spirit, Spurgeon believed that ascribing these emotions or feelings to the Spirit was proof that the Spirit must be a person, since "it must be a person who can be grieved, vexed, or resisted."[53] How these emotions could be truly applied to the Holy Spirit and God be impassible is a reality that remained a mystery to Spurgeon.

Conclusion

In 1891 Spurgeon gave the presidential address entitled *The Greatest Fight in the World* at his Pastor's College conference. For the final point in his three-point message he emphasised the person and work of the Holy Spirit. Spurgeon's placement of discussing the Holy Spirit third was not last in descending order of importance, but rather emphatically final: "Our third theme is

---

50. *MTP* 28.158.

51. *MTP* 28.159.

52. *MTP* 28.157.

53. *NPSP* 1.28.

of main importance, and though we place it last, we rank it first."[54] This section of the sermon described what the Spirit promises, sets, sanctions, blesses, and accomplishes. Each explanation of what the Spirit does assumes and requires the work of a personal being. Thus, Spurgeon asserted, "Never call the Holy Spirit 'it'; nor speak of him as if he were a doctrine, or an influence, or an orthodox myth. Reverence him, love him, and trust him with familiar yet reverent confidence. He is God, let him be God to you."[55] This presidential address captured concisely what Spurgeon spent a lifetime of ministry confirming—that the Holy Spirit can teach, has a will, possesses personal power, and can be grieved. Based on the biblical witness to these attributes, Spurgeon affirmed and defended the personhood of the Holy Spirit.

54. GFW 9.

55. GFW 57.

3

"The Mysterious Spirit"
Deity of the Holy Spirit

Brethren … let us, who are believers in Christ, view the mysterious Spirit with deep awe and reverence.[1]

Spurgeon's favorite biblical metaphor for the Holy Spirit was the comparison of the Spirit to the wind. When he preached on the topic of the Spirit and the wind, he often illustrated his point by describing the ways in which the wind provided and promoted life on earth, such as ships that are driven and moved by the wind, a farmer separating wheat from chaff by tossing the bundle into the air, and removing dust from a forgotten painting to reveal the hidden beauty. To Spurgeon, the Spirit was, as the wind to the earth, indispensable for human life and flourishing. In his February 2, 1888 sermon on John 3:8, Spurgeon urged, "Imagine a world without winds! Why, we should soon stagnate into death."[2] In another sermon on John 3:8, he illustrated this point by describing a Swiss valley between "Martigny to Bretagne" where "you will see hundreds of persons diseased … the reason is, that the air does not circulate.… There is no ventilation between the two parts of the giant Alps."[3] Spurgeon reasoned that if ever the wind would blow through that valley the people living there would find their air purified and health returned. In the same way, according to Spurgeon, the work of the Holy Spirit was life

---

1. *MTP* 10.338.
2. *MTP* 35.69.
3. *MTP* 11.351–52.

giving. The Spirit empowered creation and brought order from the ensuing chaos. The Spirit was the breath of life in human beings and gave life to the body of Jesus Christ. The Scriptures exist by the breath of God, and by them the Spirit heals Christians from their spiritual diseases.

Most significantly Spurgeon employed this imagery to affirm the Scripture's claim of the divinity of the Holy Spirit. Spurgeon believed that the Holy Spirit shared in the divine nature of the Triune God and, as such, was to be known and worshiped as God. Without a doubt, the divinity of the Holy Spirit was supported through the historical creeds that Spurgeon heartedly endorsed as true. However, the most compelling argument for the Spirit's divine nature was, to Spurgeon, the biblical comparison of the Spirit to the wind. For Spurgeon, this biblical metaphor best captured the true and mysterious nature of the Spirit's work as it demonstrated that the Holy Spirit operates as God, works according to his own will, accomplishes activity that only God can accomplish, and, therefore, is to be worshiped with the reverence due to God as he shares equally and eternally in the divine nature with the Father and the Son.

The Spirit as the Wind

Amid the numerous uses of this metaphor throughout his sermons, Spurgeon preached five sermons in which the metaphor was featured in the sermon's title.[4] In May 1877, he explained, "The metaphor of the wind cannot fully set forth the Holy Spirit, as you know ... still the wind is a most instructive metaphor as far as it goes."[5] Because Spurgeon found so much meaning in this metaphor, he admitted, "We cannot draw forth all its teaching in one sermon."[6] Thus, he often returned to this topic in his preaching. In his sermon on December 13, 1857, at Surrey Garden,

---

4. For sermons with the wind metaphor contained in the sermon's title, see *MTP* 11, sermon 630, "The Holy Spirit Compared to the Wind"; *MTP* 23, sermon 1356, "The Heavenly Wind"; *MTP* 27, sermon 1619, "The Pentecostal Wind and Fire"; *MTP* 35, sermon 2067, "The Spirit and the Wind"; *MTP* 38, sermon 2246, "Come from the Four Winds, O Breath!"

5. *MTP* 23.303.

6. *MTP* 23.303.

he preached on the necessity of the Holy Spirit for the church, and highlighted the comparison of the Spirit to the wind as one of four key biblical images of the Holy Spirit's work. When explaining the meaning of the metaphor, Spurgeon considered the exchange between Jesus and Nicodemus (John 3:1–21), the work of the Holy Spirit in Acts, and Ezekiel's encounter with the Lord in the valley of dry bones (Ezek. 37:1–14). These three references summarised Spurgeon's biblical argument for the divinity of the Holy Spirit from this biblical description of the nature of the Spirit.

First, among the five key sermons with the Spirit-wind metaphor, three were on John 3:8.[7] Jesus's reference to the Holy Spirit operating like the wind was, to Spurgeon, the most compelling argument from Scripture for the Spirit's divinity. In the earliest of Spurgeon's three sermons on John 3:8, he explained, "I selected my text with the intention of fixing upon one great illustration, which strikes me just now as being so suggestive."[8] The fact that the Holy Spirit, like the wind, "bloweth where it listeth" was, for Spurgeon, an indication of the Spirit's sovereignty to give new birth to a Christian. As such, Spurgeon reasoned, "Surely [Jesus] meant to show us that the operations of the Spirit are like the wind for *divinity*."[9] To be reconciled to God, a person must be born again, and the work of the new birth, as Spurgeon understood it, was a work completely dependent on the Holy Spirit. For example, Spurgeon questioned:

> Why has the Reformation taken root in England and among the northern nations of Europe, while in Spain and Italy it has left scarce a trace? Why blows the Holy Spirit here and not there?… Among the nations where the Spirit of God is at work how is it that he blesseth one man and not another? How is it that of two men hearing the same sermon, and subject to the same influences at home, one is taken and the other left?

---

7. *MTP* 11, sermon 630; *MTP* 23, sermon 1356; and *MTP* 35, sermon 2067.

8. *MTP* 11.277.

9. *MTP* 11.279.

Spurgeon's own answer to his questions was that the Spirit worked intentionally, not arbitrarily, according to his sovereign will. Likewise, in his May 27, 1877 sermon, Spurgeon elaborated on the freedom that the Spirit possesses to move and work as he wills, because he is "the Spirit of the living God: he is in the highest sense a free agent."[10] Indeed, eleven years later and still reflecting on this text, Spurgeon praised, "Let us adore the third Person of the Trinity in Unity, and think of him often with deep reverence in our spirits, so that we never go to work, nor to prayer, nor even to the singing of a hymn, without seeking that he would himself be the life of the holy engagement."[11] The freedom and sovereignty of the Holy Spirit to give new life to a person, as shown in John 3:8, was the bedrock for Spurgeon's defence of the deity of the Holy Spirit.

Second, the work ascribed to the Holy Spirit throughout the book of Acts was, to Spurgeon, foundational for the Spirit's later work, and fundamental for a defence of the Spirit's divinity. Spurgeon understood the coming of the Spirit in Acts as an historical event in salvation history, and as an event in which "we may learn something concerning his operations at the present time."[12] Preaching from Acts 2:2–4, the coming of the Holy Spirit at Pentecost, Spurgeon described, "The gift of the Comforter was not temporary, and the display of his power was not to be once seen and no more. The Holy Ghost is here, and we ought to expect his divine working among us."[13] The events described in Acts 2, then, displayed "plainly the power of the Holy Spirit" as he caused the gospel of God to move in power, leading to the true worship of God, providing steadfastness to his disciples, and causing the work of God to increase on earth.[14] According to Spurgeon, the coming of the Spirit at Pentecost "sets forth the fact that the true Spirit, the Spirit of God, neither comes from this place nor that, neither can his power be controlled or directed

---

10. *MTP* 23.305.

11. *MTP* 35.53.

12. *MTP* 27.521.

13. *MTP* 27.522.

14. *MTP* 27.521–22.

by human authority, but his working is ever from above, from God himself."[15] Therefore, "the work of the Holy Spirit is, so to speak, the breath of God, and his power is evermore in a special sense the immediate power of God."[16] For Spurgeon, the biblical description of the Holy Spirit's work in Acts was a demonstration of the Spirit's divinity.

Third, Spurgeon believed that the account in Ezekiel of the valley of dry bones was a depiction of the Spirit's work in regeneration, and a cause for worshiping the Holy Spirit with a reverence due to God alone. In December 1857, Spurgeon made a brief reference to Ezekiel's encounter with God in the valley of dry bones, but then he returned to the passage thirty-three years later to preach a full sermon. His understanding of that passage, as exemplified in the 1890 sermon, was focused on a spiritual reading of the text. This passage of Scripture displayed "a picture of the recovery of ungodly men from their spiritual death and corruption—a parable of the way in which sinners are brought up from their hopeless, spiritually dead condition, and made to live by the power of the Holy Ghost."[17] In this interpretation, the passage displayed the work of "that divine Spirit who becomes a Comforter to all those to whom he has been first a Quickener!"[18] Spurgeon understood the Lord's use of "wind" in Ezekiel 37:9— "Thus saith the Lord God; Come from the four winds, O breath, and breathe upon these slain, that they may live"—as a direct reference to the Holy Spirit. In Ezekiel's encounter, dry bones were enfleshed as the Spirit of God breathed life into them. In the same way, Spurgeon desired that the Holy Spirit would give new life to his listeners. Knowing that "all the power is of God alone" to accomplish this task, Spurgeon affirmed, "it is the Holy Spirit who will do it, and he only."[19] Therefore, ascribing these divine operations to the Holy Spirit, three times in that sermon

---

15. *MTP* 27.523.

16. *MTP* 27.523.

17. *MTP* 38.110.

18. *MTP* 38.110.

19. *MTP* 38.112, 118.

Spurgeon referred to the Spirit as "God the Holy Spirit."[20] Given his understanding that the Holy Spirit accomplishes regeneration for God's people, and that this is an action only God can accomplish, Spurgeon believed that the Spirit's work depicted in Ezekiel 37:1–14 affirmed the Spirit's divinity.

Conclusion

Considering the work of the Spirit of God described as the divine wind, Spurgeon praised, "Let us not mention the name of the Holy Spirit without due honor. For ever blessed be thou, most glorious Spirit, co-equal and co-eternal with the Father and with the Son; let all the angels of God worship thee! Be thou had in honor, world without end!"[21] To Spurgeon, the clearest demonstration of the Holy Spirit's divinity was the biblical comparison of the Spirit to the wind.

---

20. *MTP* 38.116, 118, 119.

21. *MTP* 11.278.

Part II

The Work of the Holy Spirit

4

"Superintending Editor"
The Holy Spirit and Scripture

> This Book contains the Word of God, and is the Word of God.…
> Blessed be the Holy Spirit for deigning to use so many writers,
> and yet himself to remain the veritable Author of this collection
> of holy books. We are grateful for Moses, for David, for Isaiah, for
> Paul, for Peter, for John, but most of all for that superintending
> Editor, that innermost Author of the whole sacred volume—even
> the Holy Ghost.[1]

Spurgeon was a voracious reader. By the end of his life he had
amassed a personal library of 12,000 volumes, in addition to
the many other books he read throughout his life. Yet the one
book that he knew he could not live without was the Bible: "As
for us, we cast anchor in the haven of the Word of God. Here
is our peace, our strength, our life, our motive, our hope, our
happiness. God's Word is our ultimatum."[2] Spurgeon's mind was
saturated with Scripture, his life as a Christian revolved around
Scripture, and his preaching was entirely dependent on Scripture.
He treasured the Bible because he knew that, in Scripture,
God was pleased to reveal himself and provide everything the
Christian needs for faith in Jesus Christ and living in a way that
honors the Lord. More specifically, Spurgeon believed that the
Holy Spirit provides this revelation through the inspiration and
illumination of Scripture. Through the testimony of Scripture a

---

1. *MTP* 37.232.
2. *GFW* 11.

person can hear, know, understand, and believe the truth about God. Yet, as Spurgeon described, a person can only come to this belief insofar as the Holy Spirit has inspired the writing, and then illumines the text so that the mind of the person is enlightened for understanding. First, this chapter will show the high value that Spurgeon placed on Scripture. Then, the following two sections will expound Spurgeon's understanding of the Spirit's work in inspiring and illuminating Scripture.

Scripture as Divine Revelation

Three months before his twenty-first birthday, Spurgeon settled any doubts about his view of the veracity and nature of Scripture: "This is the book untainted by any error, but is pure, unalloyed, perfect truth."[3] He believed that through the reading of Scripture men and women could be drawn to Jesus Christ, and Christians could be made to be more like Christ. Nevertheless, the efficacy was not in the written words alone, but in the Holy Spirit, who inspired, illuminated, and worked through the words. For Spurgeon, there was an intimate and indivisible relationship between the Spirit and the Scriptures. In his sermon titled "The Leading of the Spirit" on Romans 8:14, Spurgeon argued, "The word, as we have it printed in the Bible, is the great instrument in the hand of the Spirit for leading the children of God in the right way.… if you are led by the word of God the Spirit of God is with the word, and works through it, and you are led by the Spirit of God."[4] Therefore, Spurgeon believed that written Scripture is a tool in the hand of the Holy Spirit, which he uses to lead and guide the Christian.

Moreover, Spurgeon believed that the content of Scripture was the revelation of the living God. In a Thursday evening sermon on February 26, 1891, less than a year prior to his death and eight months to the day before he departed for the final time to Mentone, Spurgeon urged, "There is as much inspiration in this Book as when it was first penned. It is still inspired; and he that reads it aright, still feels its inspiring influence, as God

---

3. *NPSP* 1.112.
4. *MTP* 21.127–28.

comes into his heart through his own Word. The Spirit of God in the Book, and through the Book, is not straitened."[5] Spurgeon believed that the Scriptures were the work of the Triune God revealing himself to human beings. He affirmed, "The doctrine of the Trinity is especially taught in Holy Scripture."[6] God made himself known through the Scriptures, and that work of self-revelation was accomplished through the direct agency of the Holy Spirit. Spurgeon affirmed and treasured the Scriptures because he believed that God revealed himself in them, and that the Holy Spirit used the text to accomplish his work toward the Christian.

Inspiration of Scripture

Prime Minister William Gladstone (1809–1898) is credited with saying, "I have known 95 great men of the world in my time, and of these, 87 were followers of the Bible."[7] Certainly, Evangelicalism held significant cultural influence in Victorian England. Yet, this same period witnessed a rapid rise in atheism and agnosticism, creating a mood of skepticism toward the Christian faith, and leading to the loss of core tenets of Evangelicalism such as the authority and inspiration of the Bible. For example, it then became common to say that "*the word of God is in the Bible,* instead of *the word of God is the Bible.*"[8] In a time of marked cultural doubt regarding the true nature of Scripture, Spurgeon held firmly to the classic Christian view of the truthfulness, divine authorship, and authority of the Bible.

First, Spurgeon attributed the creation and content of Scripture to the work of the Holy Spirit. In February of 1855, Spurgeon began to preach regularly at Exeter Hall, and less than two months into his time preaching there, on March 18, 1855, he preached a sermon entitled, "The Bible." The first question concerning the

---

5. *MTP* 37.439.

6. *NPSP* 4.289.

7. *No Greater Love: An Edition of The Living New Testament, from The Living Bible Paraphrased* (Colorado Springs: Bibles for the World, 1984).

8. Owen Chadwick, *The Victorian Church* (New York: Oxford University Press, 1970), II.110 (emphasis added).

Bible that Spurgeon addressed was, "Who is the author?"[9] He went through the canon of Scripture naming various authors: Moses, Solomon, Micah, Amos, Hosea, Matthew, Mark, Luke, John, Paul, Peter, and James. He acknowledged the authorship of each of these men. At the same time, Spurgeon explained that the Bible "is the writing of the living God: each letter was penned with an Almighty finger; each word in it dropped from the everlasting lips, each sentence was dictated by the Holy Spirit."[10] The Scriptures were, to Spurgeon, the written word of God dictated by the Spirit.

The phrase "dictated by the Holy Spirit" was an intentional and meaningful one for Spurgeon. He understood Scripture as the sixty-six books of the Old and New Testaments, in which God's true word was delivered by human beings. Nevertheless, he explained that while Moses wrote the histories, "God guided that pen," while David produced many Psalms, "God moved his hands over the living strings of his golden harp," and when Solomon brought forth canticles of love and wisdom, "God directed his lips, and made the Preacher eloquent."[11] Naming the human authors, Spurgeon summarised that "the words are God's words, the words of the Eternal, the Invisible, the Almighty, the Jehovah of this earth. This Bible is God's Bible."[12] While Spurgeon affirmed that human beings penned the writings of Scripture, he understood that the Holy Spirit was the true author. In his preface to the 1855 reprint of the London Baptist Confession of Faith, Spurgeon urged his congregation to "Cleave fast to the Word of God... that which is manifestly approved of [Jesus Christ], and owned by the Holy Spirit."[13] Spurgeon believed that the Holy Spirit authored the Scriptures, which reveal the Triune God and attest to the person of Jesus Christ. Ultimately, the inspired words of Scripture "are not those of Moses, or David, or Paul, or Peter, but the solemn utterances of the Holy Ghost speaking

---

9. *NPSP* 1.110.
10. *NPSP* 1.110.
11. *NPSP* 1.110.
12. *NPSP* 1.110.
13. *Autobiography* 2.160–61.

through them."[14] The Spirit, then, was the divine agent who owns Scripture, having dictated its content.

Illumination of Scripture

Spurgeon believed that a person can only know and believe in Jesus through Scripture, and it is the unique role of the Holy Spirit to make the Scripture known in order to accomplish that end. Therefore, the Holy Spirit is as essential in the illumination of Scripture as in the inspiration of Scripture. First, this section will show that Spurgeon believed the Scriptures were necessary to the Christian, and the Spirit was necessary for the Scriptures to be known. Second, this section will demonstrate Spurgeon's belief that the Holy Spirit leads a Christian into new life in Christ by illuminating the Scripture.

The Necessity of Scripture

In his ministry, Spurgeon relied on the Scriptures because he understood them as necessary to the Christian and to the church. His reliance on Scripture can be seen through his work in the Pastors' College. The Pastors' College began in 1856 with one student, Thomas W. Medhurst. By 1873, attendance at the College had grown such that a new facility was needed to accommodate the student population. Plans were drawn, and on October 14 the foundation stone for the new building was laid. Halfway through construction, in March 1874, Spurgeon gave his annual College Address.[15] In the opening line of his talk, "The Need of Decision for the Truth," Spurgeon stated axiomatically, "Some things are true and some things are false."[16] However, he admitted about that proverbial saying, "[T]here are many persons who evidently do not believe it. The current principle of the present age seems to be, 'Some things are either true or false, according to the point of view from which you look at them.'"[17] Spurgeon's talk was a defence of the biblical truths essential to the Christian

---

14. *MTP* 20.122.
15. *ST* 4.38–52.
16. *ST* 4.38.
17. *ST* 4.38.

gospel, such as the doctrines of the Trinity, the atonement, the personality and divinity of the Holy Spirit, the necessity of the new birth, the evil of sin, and justification by faith. Toward the end of his address, Spurgeon inquired, "Why should we at this particular age be decided and bold?"[18] He answered, "We should be so because this age is a doubting age.... Everybody is doubting everything, not merely in religion but in politics and in social economics, in everything indeed."[19] The only proper response, he urged, was to "go back to the radix, or root of truth, and stand sternly by that which God has revealed, and so meet the wavering of the age."[20] In that "era of progress," as Spurgeon explained in his March 10, 1889 sermon, the Holy Spirit must guide men and women into the inspired Scriptures to reveal the truth:

> Dear young believers, you who wish to understand the Scriptures, seek this light from above, for this is the true light. Other lights may mislead, but this is clear and sure. To have the Spirit of God lighting up the inner chambers of truth, is a great boon. Truth of the deeper sort is comparable to a cavern, into which we cannot find our way except by a guide and a light. When the Spirit of truth is come, he pours daylight into the darkness, and leads us into all truth. He does not merely show the truth, but he leads us into it, so that we stand within it, and rejoice in the hid treasure which it contains. Then we know him as our sacred illuminator.[21]

The Holy Spirit was, to Spurgeon, the sacred illuminator of Scripture, which was the needed source of truth in an age of skepticism.

The Mysterious Work of Illumination

Spurgeon was convinced that owning and reading a Bible was not enough for a person to know God; rather, the text must be illuminated by the mysterious work of the Holy Spirit for it to accomplish its aim of regenerating, converting, sanctifying, and sustaining the Christian. In his November 18, 1855 sermon,

18. *ST* 4.47.
19. *ST* 4.47.
20. *ST* 4.47–48.
21. *MTP* 35.137.

Spurgeon asked, "Now, have any of you an illuminated Bible at home?"[22] He described illumination as "the best way in which the Holy Ghost leads us into all truth."[23] One may read the Bible "to all eternity, and never learn anything by it, unless it is illuminated by the Spirit."[24] Spurgeon believed that in order for a person to comprehend Scripture, the Spirit must work effectually, which was a mysterious work in the Christian's mind.

Spurgeon had experienced this mysterious work of the Spirit firsthand in his life and ministry. When Spurgeon was a boy, the travelling village preacher Richard Knill visited Stambourne and spoke prophetically that Spurgeon would one day preach at Rowland Hill's church.[25] Knill then gave young Charles a sixpence earnest payment to keep a promise that when he preached at that chapel William Cowper's song "God Moves in a Mysterious Way" must be sung. Not long after Spurgeon arrived in London, he preached the annual children's sermon at Surrey Chapel, and kept the agreement by having the children sing Cowper's hymn. The final verse of the hymn announces, "Blind unbelief is sure to err // And scan His work in vain; // God is His own interpreter, // And He will make it plain."[26] Indeed, Spurgeon trusted that God was his own interpreter. Whether this sovereign work of God related to his providential ordering of history (as in Cowper's song), the reasons for which would one day be made clear, or whether this sovereign interpretation referred to God's use and intentions through Scripture, Spurgeon believed the Spirit moved and worked as he so willed.

Specifically in relation to Scripture, Spurgeon believed that it was the unique role of the Holy Spirit to take the words of the Bible and make them known and believed in a person's mind and heart. Thus, in his sermon at Surrey Chapel Spurgeon praised, "Oh, it is a blessed thing to read an illuminated Bible lit up by the radiance of the Holy Ghost.... The book seems made of gold

---

22.   *NPSP* 1.384.

23.   *NPSP* 1.384.

24.   *NPSP* 1.385.

25.   For the story of Richard Knill's prophecy, see *Autobiography* 1.33–38.

26.   *Hymnbook* 211.

leaf; every single letter glitters like a diamond."[27] In Spurgeon's own life the Lord moved in mysterious ways. From a humble prayer and a sixpence down payment, the Holy Spirit caused the Scriptures to glitter like a diamond in Spurgeon's mind. He also knew that the Spirit must work to illuminate the Scriptures if they were to appear to a person like golden-leafed pages.

Conclusion

In August of 1890, after a lifetime of ministry, Spurgeon summarised his view on Scripture, "No man's voice is to be sovereign to you; but only the voice of God the Holy Spirit, speaking out of this Book, which contains all things that you need for life and godliness. May God the Holy Ghost give you grace to fetch all your instructions from it!"[28] The Scripture was the treasured source of truth in Spurgeon's life and ministry because its very words were dictated by the Holy Spirit. Spurgeon believed that the Spirit inspired and illumined the text of Scripture, and, as such, Scripture was the Holy Spirit's chief instrument for accomplishing his work in the Christian.

---

27. *NPSP* 1.385.
28. *MTP* 38.519.

5

"Master Artist"
The Holy Spirit and Creation

The first divine act in fitting up this planet for the habitation of man was for the Spirit of God to move upon the face of the waters. Till that time all was formless, empty, out of order and in confusion. In a word, it was chaos; and to make it into that thing of beauty which the world is at the present moment, even though it is a fallen world, it was needful that the movement of the Spirit of God would take place upon it.... [I]n this great picture of material beauty we may see the handiwork of that ... Master Artist.[1]

Spurgeon marvelled at the created universe. When not engaged with ministry work, his two favorite activities were reading books and observing nature, and his two most preferred reading topics were, first, biblical and theological books and, second, books on the subject of the natural world. When his wife Susannah was commenting on the pictures of Spurgeon's library at Westwood she remembered, "One whole bay is filled with works on natural history and the sciences."[2] Spurgeon had a deep appreciation for the created world. He would be led to the praise of God for creating such a world, and his preaching was filled with illustrations from his observations and readings of the physical universe. He received without question the biblical witness that all things were created by God, and he believed that

---

1. *MTP* 55.109–110.
2. *Autobiography* 4.290.

the Holy Spirit was the person of the Godhead who empowered the work of creation. While he confessed that the creation event was a Trinitarian work, he also believed that at creation it was the Spirit who produced the substance of the universe and brought order out of the ensuing chaos. Similarly, Spurgeon affirmed that the creation event was an historical event, and at the same time, he interpreted the biblical account of creation spiritually as prefiguring the later work of the Spirit described in Scripture. In this way, the Spirit's operations of producing and ordering the material substance of the universe mirrored the Spirit's future work of regenerating, converting, sanctifying, and preserving the Christian. Though creation itself remained insufficient for one to know and believe the Christian gospel, by the agency of the Holy Spirit the created world witnessed to the reality of God and provided insights into God's character and work. Thus, while Spurgeon affirmed that the Spirit revealed God authoritatively through Scripture, he also believed that the Spirit's work in creation was the most helpful illustration for understanding Scripture and understanding how the Spirit works in the life of the Christian.

Creation as a Trinitarian Event

Spurgeon argued that the work of creation was a Trinitarian event. While he understood that Scripture attributed the power and work of creation to the person of the Holy Spirit, he also recognised that in various places the Bible also attributed the work to the Father and to the Son.[3] As Spurgeon celebrated in an 1891 sermon, "Come, then, rejoice with the Father, rejoice with the Son, rejoice with the Spirit; and if the Lord God, as the Trinity in Unity, invites us to be glad and rejoice in that which he creates, let us not hold back."[4] Spurgeon recognised the biblical witness to the Trinitarian nature of creation, and, as with his pneumatology

---

3. See *NPSP* 1.230. Relevant biblical passages include, for example, Isaiah 45:7, Malachi 2:10, John 1:1–3, Ephesians 3:9, Colossians 1:15–16, Hebrews 1:2, and Revelation 4:11.

4. *MTP* 37.360.

in general, his depiction of the Spirit's work in creation existed within a Trinitarian framework.

An Historical and Spiritualised Hermeneutic of Creation

While Spurgeon spiritualised the Old Testament accounts of creation, he maintained the historicity of the creation events described in the biblical text, contrary to the methodological naturalism that was modifying the way the Bible was read and interpreted in Spurgeon's day. Spurgeon's historical and spiritualised reading can be seen in his 1865 sermon at Cornwall Baptist Chapel and in his description of the Holy Spirit's particular work of bringing order out of the chaos of creation. First, in 1863 Spurgeon's brother, James Archer Spurgeon, became the first minister at Cornwall Baptist Chapel and served in that capacity for four years until he was requested to take on more responsibility at the Pastors' College to relieve Charles from many of the leadership duties.[5] While James was at Cornwall Chapel, his brother preached to that congregation on at least three separate occasions.[6] On November 12, 1865, Charles preached a sermon for his brother titled "Light, Natural and Spiritual." Preaching at a newly formed church that was experiencing ministry growth and new birth, Spurgeon was drawn to the biblical description of God's work in creation. Nonetheless, while the sermon text was Genesis 1:1–5, Spurgeon explained that "the first creation is not the subject of this morning's discourse: *we would rather direct your minds to the second creation of God.*"[7] Instead of giving a detailed explanation of creation, Spurgeon highlighted the "great work which Jesus Christ is accomplishing in the world, by the Holy Spirit through the Word," in making all things new.[8] In his spiritualised reading, the moving of the Spirit over the waters showed that the "secret work of the Holy Spirit begins in

---

5. William Pepperell, *The Church Index: A Book of Metropolitan Churches and Church Enterprise—Part I. Kensington* (London: W. Wells Gardner, 1872), 50–51.

6. *MTP* 9, sermon 537; *MTP* 11, sermon 660; *MTP* 12, sermon 698. Charles also preached at the 1867 inauguration service of James's successor, Rev. Charles White (Pepperell, 51).

7. *MTP* 11.637 (emphasis added).

8. *MTP* 11.637.

the human heart.... The Holy Ghost mysteriously quickens the dead heart, excites emotions, longings, desires."[9] Again, the first "divine fiat" of God's creation of light was illustrative for showing that "unless the light of his Spirit has revealed [Jesus] to you as the great substitute for sinners.... You know him not."[10] In Spurgeon's spiritualised hermeneutic of Genesis 1:1–5, the ultimate point of the text was to depict the work of the Spirit toward the Christian.

Nevertheless, Spurgeon's emphasis on the Spirit's work in giving new life to the Christian was not at the expense of his belief in the historicity of the creation account. Spurgeon opened the sermon at Cornwall Chapel by clarifying, "This is, no doubt, a literal and accurate account of God's first day's work in the creation of the world."[11] In this way, Spurgeon explained, "We believe the old creation to have been typical of the new."[12] Therefore, he understood that in both creation and new creation, the "Spirit works mysteriously and silently, but most efficaciously."[13] In a sermon ten years earlier, Spurgeon similarly argued, "[I]f you will look in the 1st chapter of Genesis, you will there see more particularly set forth that peculiar operation of power upon the universe which was put forth by the Holy Spirit; you will then discover what was his special work."[14] Spurgeon recognised that the material universe and all life on earth was a direct work of the Holy Spirit. "The creation of the heavens above us," Spurgeon explained, "and the creation of all life and all flesh... is said to be a work of God's Spirit."[15] Even with his spiritualised reading of the creation account, Spurgeon maintained the historical accuracy of the events described in Genesis 1–2. For Spurgeon, the Holy Spirit was the active agent in creation, which also showed how the Spirit creates new life in the Christian.

---

9.   *MTP* 11.638.
10. *MTP* 11.638.
11. *MTP* 11.637.
12. *MTP* 11.637.
13. *MTP* 11.638.
14. *NPSP* 1.230.
15. *NPSP* 1.230.

Second, Spurgeon's hermeneutic of creation can be seen in his description of the Spirit's work of bringing order out of chaos. The Holy Spirit was involved in creating the matter that makes up the universe, though, according to Spurgeon, the Spirit's more particular work was to organise the created substance in order for life to exist. Spurgeon was uncertain of the age of the earth and the length of time between the initial creation depicted in the first half of Genesis 1:2 and the Spirit's ordering of it for life in the second half of Genesis 1:2. As Spurgeon indicated in 1855, "We know not how remote the period of the creation of this globe may be—certainly many millions of years before the time of Adam."[16] Before the Spirit hovered over the face of the waters, according to Spurgeon, the planet had "passed through various stages of existence, and different kinds of creatures have lived on its surface, all of which have been fashioned by God.... He allowed the inward fires to burst up from beneath and melt all the solid matter, so that all kinds of substances were commingled in one vast mass of disorder."[17] Unable to describe what creation looked like at that time, Spurgeon admitted that "the only name you could give to the world then was, that it was a chaotic mass of matter."[18] Spurgeon believed this period of creation existed prior to the time "wherein man should be its principal tenant and monarch."[19] Then, when the Spirit moved over the confused mass "all the different portions of matter came into their places, and it was no longer 'without form, and void;' but became round like its sister planets, and moved, singing the high praises of God—not discordantly as it had done before, but as one great note in the vast scale of creation."[20] Spurgeon upheld the historical reality and significance of the Spirit's ordering of creation.

Moreover, the work of the Spirit to bring order out of the chaos of creation was as mysterious to Spurgeon as the work of the Spirit to give new life to a Christian. As he described on January

---

16. *NPSP* 1.230.

17. *NPSP* 1.230.

18. *NPSP* 1.230.

19. *NPSP* 1.230.

20. *NPSP* 1.230.

23, 1873, "Ever must the contact of the Spirit with materialism remain a marvel."[21] For Spurgeon, only the Spirit could bring "order where there was nought but confusion," and he did so by "the simple spreading of his dove-like wings."[22] The imagery of bringing order to chaos struck Spurgeon as the same work of the Holy Spirit to bring order to a person's chaotic life of sin. Whereas sin leads to disorder the Spirit brought order, and just as the Spirit worked on the chaotic mass of matter so too he worked to bring life to the new Christian. Spurgeon's marvelling at the natural world was ultimately a marvelling at the work of the Spirit in new creation, for all of this "is the power of the Spirit."[23] To Spurgeon, the Holy Spirit's particular work was to bring order out of the chaos of creation, an operation that was depicted in the Spirit's work to give new life to the Christian. In all, Spurgeon's reading of the Old Testament maintained Scripture's historicity, though he identified the climax of the Spirit's work in creation as giving new life to the Christian.

Creation as Illustrative of Scripture

While Spurgeon believed that the "Master Artist" of creation was the Holy Spirit, he also maintained that there was an essential relationship between the Spirit's work in creation and in inspiring the Scriptures. The Holy Spirit was the active agent of God in creation, and through the created world he provided insight into Scripture. Thus, Spurgeon often illustrated or explained Scripture with examples from the natural world. For example, Spurgeon encouraged preachers to study the created world for insights into God and illustrations of Scripture. In volume two of *Lectures to My Students*, Spurgeon reckoned, "Most of us have read Alphonse Karr's book, *A Tour Round My Garden*."[24] In that book, French journalist Jean-Baptiste Alphonse Karr provided proverbial

---

21.   *MTP* 55.112.

22.   *NPSP* 1.231.

23.   *NPSP* 1.230.

24.   *Lectures* 2.64.

wisdom drawn from his observations of the natural world.[25] In Letter LV, Karr observed the uselessness of the groundsel laurel to a human being. From this observation, he argued that human beings were not the centre of existence, even though many perceived themselves to be. Having lived through two French revolutions and seen no remedy in the continued struggle against human inequality, Karr lamented, "The more frequently things change, the more they continue to be the same thing."[26]

With Karr, Spurgeon commended the method of illustrating from nature; however, he urged his students to study the natural world for insights into its Creator, not merely for proverbial wisdom, since:

> There is a touch of the divine finger in all that God has made; so that the things which are apparent to our senses have certain resemblances to the things which do not appear. That which can be seen, and tasted, and touched, and handled, is meant to be to us the outward and visible sign of a something which we find in the Word of God, and in our spiritual experience, which is the inward and the spiritual grace; so that there is nothing forced and unnatural in bringing nature to illustrate grace; it was ordained of God for that very purpose.[27]

Spurgeon believed that "the Author of revelation" was also "the Author of creation, and providence, and history," so that, "When you use natural history to illustrate the Scriptures, you are only explaining one of God's books by another volume that he has written."[28] Thus, a Christian preacher should draw from "geology, astronomy, botany, or any of the other sciences which will help to shed a side light upon the Scriptures."[29] Spurgeon's natural theology was grounded by Scripture and rooted in his belief that

---

25. Alphonse Karr, *A Tour Round My Garden*, trans. J. G. Wood (London: G. Routledge, & Co., 1855). Wood described that Karr "treats a sham much like an American Indian treats an enemy—he tomahawks him with an argument, scalps him with an epigram, and triumphantly despoils him of his borrowed plumes" (vii).

26. Karr, *A Tour*, 313. The quotation is J. G. Wood's translation of the French phrase, "Plus ça change, plus c'est la même chose."

27. *Lectures* 3.63.

28. *Lectures* 3.63.

29. *Lectures* 3.64.

the Holy Spirit was the personal and direct agent of creation. He believed that observations of the natural world were theologically instructive because creation was the work of the Holy Spirit who revealed God through the sacred texts of Scripture.

Further, for Spurgeon, observing the natural world was not only an investigation into God, but could lead to communion with the Creator. It was understandable that Spurgeon would possess, among his fellow city dwellers, a heightened awareness of the beauty of creation. He was the "Essex bumpkin" who had come to the metropolis.[30] His tastes were attuned to the artist of nature over and against the architecture of the city. Unlike other busy urbanites, Spurgeon took time to look at the clouds and contemplate nature. In his sermon on August 19, 1855, Spurgeon preached, "Wherever I look abroad in nature I love to discern my Father's name spelled out in living characters; and if we had any fields a little greener than Moorfields, Smithfield, and Spafields, I would do as Isaac did, go into the fields at eventide and muse and meditate upon the God of nature."[31] Despite his desire for more green space in the city, Spurgeon reported, "I thought in the cool of last evening I would muse with my God, by his Holy Spirit, and see what message he would give me."[32] By observing the natural world, Spurgeon was led by the Holy Spirit into communion with God.

Spurgeon rejected the idea that the science and beauty of creation were at odds with the truth of Scripture. In his 1871 sermon on Psalm 104, titled "Lessons from Nature," Spurgeon decried a trend that many people "in these modern times have thought it to be a mark of high spirituality never to observe nature."[33] Spurgeon, on the other hand, announced, "There is no quarrel between nature and revelation, fools only think so: to wise men the one illustrates and establishes the other.... Who will may neglect the volume of creation, or the volume of revelation,

---

30. William Thomas Stead, "Mr. Spurgeon at Home," *The Pall Mall Gazette*, June 18, 1884, 11.

31. *NPSP* 1.277. The title of the sermon was "What Are the Clouds?"

32. *NPSP* 1.277.

33. *MTP* 17.445.

I shall delight in them both as long as I live."[34] In a sermon on Isaiah 65:17–19, Spurgeon added, "I must confess that I think it a most right and excellent thing that you and I should rejoice in the natural creation of God."[35] Spurgeon rejoiced in and enjoyed nature because he believed that the Holy Spirit who created Scripture also communicated through the world he created. In this way, Spurgeon believed that creation was a divine aid of the Holy Spirit for understanding God's self-revelation in Scripture.

Conclusion

When Spurgeon preached on the work of creation, the epic poems of John Milton, *Paradise Lost* (1667) and *Paradise Regained* (1671), were never far from his mind.[36] Spurgeon was twenty years old, preaching a sermon on the power of the Holy Spirit, and quoted Milton's beautiful description of the Trinitarian nature of creation—"The King of Glory, in his powerful Word // And Spirit coming to create new worlds."[37] At the same time, Spurgeon was gripped by Milton's description of the Spirit's unique role in creation: "But on the watery calm // His brooding wings the Spirit of God outspread // and vital virtue infused and vital warmth // Throughout the fluid mass."[38] Sixteen years later, Spurgeon preached his sermon on Psalm 104 entitled "Lessons from Nature," again having the work of Milton on his mind. In this August 1871 sermon, Spurgeon showed how the natural world reflects the God who created it. He encouraged his congregation to look at creation

---

34. *MTP* 17.446–47.

35. *MTP* 37.351.

36. See *NPSP* 1, sermon 30; *MTP* 11, sermon 660; and *MTP* 17, sermon 1005. On September 1, 1881, Spurgeon conveyed, "I recollect how, when I began to preach the gospel, I used to wish that Milton had been a preacher. I often thought what a grand thing it would have been if Shakespeare had been a minister; with his wonderful versatility of talent, and poetry of expression, I thought he would have been a very powerful preacher. But, afterwards, I almost thanked God that we had not any Miltons or Shakespeares preaching. It is far better to have men of quite another stamp, so that the hearers may not be carried away either with poetical expressions or with an excess of worldly knowledge and ability" (*MTP* 46.465).

37. John Milton, *Paradise Lost*, ed. A. W. Verity (Cambridge: Cambridge University Press, 1910), VII.208–9. For Spurgeon's quotation, see *NPSP* 1.230.

38. Milton, *Paradise Lost*, VII.234–7. For Spurgeon's quotation, see *NPSP* 1.230. Spurgeon, in his quotation of Milton in this sermon, omitted lines VII.218–34a.

to see God, since "he who wrote the Bible, the second and clearest revelation of his divine mind, wrote also the first book, the book of nature; and who are we that we should derogate from the worth of the first because we esteem the second."[39] He celebrated Psalm 104 as "all through a song of nature, the adoration of God in the great outward temple of the universe."[40] He recognised the poetic beauty of creation in Scripture, especially as described by Milton who captured the power and beauty of the Spirit's work. For Spurgeon, the Holy Spirit was active in bringing forth the substance of creation, and especially in bringing order out of the chaos that ensued. The work of the Holy Spirit in creation was mysterious and effectual, and led Spurgeon to declare, "Only as the Spirit came did the work of creation begin."[41] Thus, according to Spurgeon, it is only by the Holy Spirit that life exists, and it is only by the Holy Spirit that a Christian can have new life in Christ.

---

39. *MTP* 17.446.
40. *MTP* 17.445.
41. *MTP* 55.109.

6

"Masterpiece of the Holy Spirit"
The Holy Spirit and Christ

Though our Lord Jesus Christ was born of a woman and made in the likeness of sinful flesh, yet the power that begat Him was entirely in God the Holy Spirit—as the Scriptures express it, "The power of the Highest shall overshadow thee." He was begotten as the Apostles' Creed says, begotten of the Holy Ghost. "That holy thing which is born of thee shall be called the Son of the Highest." The corporeal frame of the Lord Jesus Christ was a masterpiece of the Holy Spirit.[1]

The first sermon that Spurgeon ever preached was an impromptu sermon in 1851 at a small cottage in Teversham. He travelled to Teversham with a companion, each of the two young men thinking it was the other who was going to preach the sermon. By the time they realised their false assumption that the other was to preach, it was too late for either one to prepare a sermon. Spurgeon agreed to take up the task, and selected 1 Peter 2:7 as his sermon text: "Unto you therefore which believe he is precious." His hope was to preach Jesus, share the story of the cross, and "tell a few poor cottagers of the sweetness and love of Jesus."[2] Later in life, Spurgeon reflected on that first sermon and his hope to preach Christ: "This was the theme of the first

---

1. *NPSP* 1.231.
2. *Autobiography* 1.201.

sermon I ever preached, I hope it is my theme now, and ever shall be living, dying and glorified."[3]

Without doubt, Spurgeon's aim in ministry was to preach the truth about the person and work of Jesus Christ, and the result of his ministry bears witness to a man who was centrally focused toward that end. At the same time, Spurgeon believed that a proper knowledge of the person and work of Jesus Christ required a proper understanding of the person and work of the Holy Spirit. The Holy Spirit empowered the life and work of Jesus Christ, including his birth, ministry, resurrection, and ascension. The Holy Spirit made known the truth about Jesus to the apostles. The Spirit inspired the Scripture which teaches that salvation comes through Jesus Christ alone. In fact, Spurgeon described salvation as both found in Christ alone and as a work of the Holy Spirit from beginning to end. Spurgeon's dual emphases on the person and work of Jesus Christ and on that of the Holy Spirit are not competing emphases but complementary. He understood that, in and through the person and work of Jesus, the Spirit was providing the way to give new life to the Christian.

First, this chapter will demonstrate Spurgeon's understanding that the Holy Spirit empowered the incarnation and birth of Jesus Christ. Then the chapter will show that Spurgeon believed each facet of the life of Christ was accomplished in the power of the Holy Spirit.

The Holy Spirit and the Incarnation

In Spurgeon's first sermon in the Metropolitan Tabernacle, he determined that the theme of his ministry would be focused on Jesus Christ: "I would propose that the subject of the ministry of this house, as long as this platform shall stand, and as long as this house shall be frequented by worshippers, shall be the person of Jesus Christ."[4] Preaching Christ meant, for Spurgeon, affirming the "*infinite and indisputable Godhead,*" (emphasis added), the full humanity and divinity of Christ, Christ as the only mediator between God and humans, the sufficiency of the redemption of

---

3. *LS* 6.311.

4. *MTP* 7.169.

Christ, the headship of Christ over the church, and the authority of Christ as king over all things.[5] In the concluding point of his first sermon at the Metropolitan Tabernacle, Spurgeon identified the efficacy of Christ-exalting preaching as the work of the Holy Spirit, for "there is a power about this subject when it is preached with the demonstration of the Spirit."[6] Spurgeon had spoken of this power before. Fourteen months after accepting the invitation to become the pastor at New Park Street Chapel, he preached a sermon called "The Power of the Holy Ghost," where the first word of the sermon was emphatically, "Power."[7] As he outlined in that sermon, the Holy Spirit was himself the power at work to proclaim Christ. Even more, the Spirit was the one who empowered Jesus Christ as he accomplished the Father's work on earth.

As Spurgeon understood Scripture, the incarnation of Jesus Christ was a work of the Holy Spirit. On June 9, 1867, reflecting on the birth of Jesus, Spurgeon recognised, "Our Lord was born into this world through the marvelous, mysterious, secret operation of the divine Spirit."[8] It was by the work and power of the Holy Spirit that Jesus Christ was born in Bethlehem, as Spurgeon declared, "The Christ in the manger is begotten by the Holy Spirit."[9] Moreover, he imagined that Jesus could have said to the Holy Spirit, "A body hast thou prepared me."[10] Spurgeon supposed the body of Jesus "to have excelled all others in beauty," since "in all its beauty and perfection" it was "modelled by the Spirit."[11] For Spurgeon, the birth of Jesus occurred by the creative energy of the Holy Spirit, and the body of Christ was formed to be "the very pattern of what the body is to be in heaven."[12]

---

5.   *MTP* 7.170.

6.   *MTP* 7.175.

7.   *NPSP* 1.229.

8.   *MTP* 13.316.

9.   *MTP* 13.316.

10.   *MTP* 13.316.

11.   *NPSP* 1.231.

12.   *NPSP* 1.231.

The Holy Spirit and the Life and Ministry of Jesus Christ

Spurgeon also perceived that the life and ministry of Jesus were empowered by the Holy Spirit. Before explaining further, it is important to remember Spurgeon's theological commitment to the inseparability of God's operations. As we have seen earlier, Spurgeon believed that God's work was indivisible, so that an operation of any person of the divine Trinity is attributable to each person sharing in the divine nature of the Godhead. This theological perspective was especially worked out for Spurgeon in relation to the earthly ministry of Jesus. While Jesus in his divine nature possessed the divine power to accomplish divine works, Spurgeon also recognised the way that the Scripture witnessed to the work of the Holy Spirit in relation to the life and ministry of Jesus. For instance, at the water baptism of Jesus Christ, as Spurgeon understood it, the Holy Spirit consecrated Christ to his work on earth. When the Spirit descended on Jesus like a dove, Christ "was that day publicly and effectually set apart by the Holy Spirit to be distinctly the great Captain of our salvation, the Apostle and High Priest of our profession."[13] Spurgeon understood that the event was not merely Jesus's baptism in water, but his baptism in the Holy Spirit. One year earlier, reflecting on the Spirit's role in Jesus's baptism, Spurgeon observed, "It was the Spirit of God who gave success to Jesus Christ's ministry."[14] Spurgeon maintained that, beginning at Jesus's baptism, the efficacious power behind the miracles and preaching of Jesus was the Holy Spirit's operation. As such, the Holy Spirit equipped and empowered Jesus in his ministry success. Thus, Spurgeon described, "Albeit that as Deity [Jesus] could work what miracles he willed, yet he chose to use the divine power of the Holy Spirit of God in the working of many of his wonders."[15]

---

13. *MTP* 13.316–17.
14. *MTP* 58.183.
15. *MTP* 13.317.

The Holy Spirit and the Crucifixion

Moreover, Spurgeon believed that it was by the power of the Holy Spirit that Jesus Christ was enabled to lay down his life in death. In Spurgeon's September 21, 1873 sermon, he considered the "remarkable title which is here given to the Holy Spirit... 'the Spirit of Christ.'"[16] One of the key reasons for this title was that *"Christ lived peculiarly in the power of the Spirit."*[17] However, for Spurgeon, Jesus not only was born and lived in the power of the Holy Spirit, but his willingness to face death on the cross was a work of the Holy Spirit. In reading Romans 8:9, Spurgeon noticed the juxtaposition between "Spirit" and "flesh." Regarding Jesus, he described, "Never did the flesh rule Christ," but rather "every thought, desire, and aim were of the highest, noblest, and most spiritual order."[18] The flesh had no power over Jesus, since "the Spirit of holiness and love was in him, —that Spirit which brings power and peace."[19] It was by the Spirit of love that Jesus "sought not its own, but made Him lay down His life for His friends."[20]

The Holy Spirit and the Resurrection

Spurgeon also ascribed to the Holy Spirit the work of giving life to the corporeal body of Jesus Christ at the resurrection. Spurgeon recognised that Scripture sometimes refers to the resurrection of Christ as being performed by the Son's own agency, sometimes by the Father, and sometimes by the Holy Spirit. As Spurgeon explained, Jesus Christ "was raised by the Father because ... he gave an official message which delivered Jesus from the grave. He was raised by his own majesty and power because he had a right to come out.... But, he was raised by the Spirit as to that energy which his mortal frame received."[21] Spurgeon acknowledged that as Jesus "willingly gave up his life he had power to take it

---

16. *MTP* 19.530.
17. *MTP* 19.531 (emphasis added).
18. *MTP* 19.532.
19. *MTP* 19.532.
20. *MTP* 19.532.
21. *NPSP* 1.231.

again."[22] He also noticed that in Acts 13:30 and Philippians 2:9 "you find [the resurrection] ascribed to God the Father: 'He raised him up from the dead:' 'Him hath God the Father exalted.'"[23] Further, Spurgeon especially attributed to the Holy Spirit the work of transmitting new life back into the body of Jesus Christ. Given Spurgeon's belief in the inseparability of God's operations, Scripture's attribution of the resurrection to all three persons of the Godhead was not a contradiction or confusion, but rather a proper description of the Triune God at work, particularly in the resurrection of Jesus Christ.

The Holy Spirit and the Ascension

Finally, the resurrection of Jesus Christ culminated in his ascension to the right hand of the Father. For Spurgeon, as much as the ascension was focused on the raising up of Jesus, it was equally concerned with the coming down of the Holy Spirit. In January of 1888, the Downgrade Controversy came to a head—Spurgeon withdrew from the Baptist Union and the Baptist Union Council voted to censure the preacher. Three months later, in April 1888, Spurgeon also withdrew from the London Baptist Association. On the first day of that month, he preached a sermon on the conversation in Acts 25 between Festus and King Agrippa concerning the accusations against Paul. Spurgeon, commenting on the hostility in Paul's life, likely with his own hostilities in mind, exhorted,

> Let me add that *where the gospel is faithfully preached the reproach of Christ will not be shunned by the preacher....* There is no hope of preaching Christ faithfully without being called by disrespectful titles, regarded as a fool, and reckoned among the vulgar and ignorant. Some kind of ugly name will always be appended to the gospeller.[24]

---

22. *NPSP* 1.231.
23. *NPSP* 1.231.
24. *MTP* 34.186 (emphasis added).

Spurgeon conceded, "Brethren, expect it, and accept it! Bid farewell to a quiet life, if you resolve to be true to Jesus. Nothing excites such animosity as the preaching of Jesus."[25]

In response, Spurgeon put his hope in the ascended Jesus and the coming of the Holy Spirit. He explained, "Many blessings come from our Lord's death, but the Holy Spirit was an early gift of his resurrection life: especially was it the outcome of his ascended life. The gift of the Holy Spirit is the ascension gift of our living Lord."[26] Two years later, in his sermon titled "The Lord's Triumphant Ascension," Spurgeon described that in the descent of Christ the Holy Spirit prepared "that blessed body ... for the indwelling of the Second Person of the adorable Trinity."[27] In similar fashion, at the ascent of Christ, the Holy Spirit was sent down to dwell within God's people. The fullness of this event was, to Spurgeon, a Trinitarian reality: "How delightful it is to see the Trinity working out in unity the salvation of men! 'Thou hast ascended on high': there is Christ Jesus. 'Thou hast received gifts for men': there is the Father, bestowing those gifts. The gift itself is the Holy Spirit. This is the great largess of Christ's ascension."[28] The ascension was simultaneously the rising of Jesus Christ to the right hand of the Father, and the coming of the Holy Spirit to dwell within the children of God.

Conclusion

Spurgeon believed that the Holy Spirit was a part of and empowered every facet of the life and ministry of Jesus Christ. "Hence, then," as Spurgeon explained, "the Spirit of God is rightly called the Spirit of Christ."[29] Preaching to a capacity crowd at the newly renovated Metropolitan Tabernacle on June 6, 1867, Spurgeon described:

---

25. *MTP* 34.186.

26. *MTP* 34.190.

27. *MTP* 36.244.

28. *MTP* 36.247.

29. *MTP* 19.533.

See then, beloved, from the birth of Christ to his resurrection, he was pleased to put honor upon the Holy Spirit by receiving abundantly of his power. He was anointed as man with the oil of gladness above his fellows; and though able as God to have done as he pleased, independently, yet in order that the unity of the blessed Trinity might be manifest to us, Christ went not without his Father's sending, and spoke not his own words, but his Father's words; and so the power which rested upon him, which he chose to use, was the power of the Holy Ghost.[30]

Spurgeon maintained that it was by the power of the Holy Spirit that the Son of God became incarnate in Jesus Christ, lived and completed his ministry on earth, willingly became obedient to death on a cross, was raised from the dead, ascended to the right hand of the Father, and gave out the gift of the Holy Spirit to God's people. Thus, as Spurgeon explained, the person and work of Christ should always be seen in relation to the Holy Spirit, because "His life was a life in the Spirit."[31]

30. *MTP* 13.317.
31. *MTP* 19.532.

7

"Spirit of Grace"
The Holy Spirit and the Covenant of Grace

Look, again, at the covenant of grace. We know that there was a covenant made with the Lord Jesus Christ, by his Father, from before all worlds, and that in this covenant the persons of all his people were given to him, and were secured; but of what use, or of what avail is the covenant to us, until the Holy Spirit brings the blessings of the covenant to us?… What is Christ's blood to any of you, until you have received the Spirit of grace?… The Spirit is absolutely necessary. Without him neither the works of the Father, nor of the Son, are of any avail to us.[1]

In 1856, the membership at New Park Street grew to 860 people. Even with the renovated chapel, the increase in attendance overwhelmed the facility's capacity. So, on June 16, 1856, the church summoned the first meeting of the committee that would superintend the plans and construction of the Metropolitan Tabernacle.[2] In the summer of 1856, along with the appointment of the Metropolitan Tabernacle Building Committee, Spurgeon produced the first of a three-part series on the nature of the covenant of grace—"God in the Covenant," "Christ in the Covenant," and "The Holy Spirit in the Covenant."[3] While he prepared the church for a new building, he also built up his congregation in covenantal theology. In this sermon series, Spurgeon outlined the role of the Father, Son, and Holy Spirit in

---

1. *NPSP* 5.212–13.

2. See *Letters* 126. See also, *Autobiography* 2.5, 331.

3. *NPSP* 2, sermon 93; *NPSP* 2, sermon 103; and *MTP* 53, sermon 3048.

the covenant and how the people of God became recipients of the covenantal blessings.

Spurgeon's first priority in those three sermons was to highlight a covenantal hermeneutic as the essential metanarrative of Scripture. In the introduction to the first sermon, Spurgeon reflected on the nature of the covenant of grace: "What a glorious covenant the second covenant is!... It is so glorious that the very thought of it is enough to overwhelm the soul."[4] Spurgeon believed the most overwhelming part of this covenant was "the amazing condescension and infinite love of God," in which God "framed a covenant for such unworthy creatures, for such glorious purposes, with such disinterested motives."[5]

Spurgeon regularly preached sermons detailing his understanding of covenantal theology, and he maintained that, within the canonical Scriptures, there was a covenantal structure to God's relationship with humanity. In his sermon titled "The Wondrous Covenant," Spurgeon opened with "The doctrine of the divine covenant lies at the root of all true theology. It has been said that he who well understands the distinction between the covenant of works and the covenant of grace is a master of divinity."[6] Drawing from his studies of Puritan theology, Spurgeon attested that "the old Scotch divines, and our own Puritanic forefathers, were of opinion that the two covenants are the very essence of all theology."[7] As he observed a neglect among churches in his time on teachings on the covenant of grace, his remedy in his own teaching was to show the covenantal reading of Scripture as "the key of theology" and the "diamond hinges on which the golden doors of grace are made to turn."[8] For Spurgeon, a covenantal framework was the essential hermeneutic of Scripture. Therefore, his biblical theology was oriented around God's interaction with humanity through covenants.

---

4. *NPSP* 2.313.
5. *NPSP* 2.313.
6. *MTP* 58.517.
7. *MTP* 60.309.
8. *MTP* 36.468.

Spurgeon's Covenantal Framework

Spurgeon opted for the twofold approach in his covenantal reading of Scripture rather than the threefold method. The basic historical structure to covenantal theology teaches either a twofold or threefold approach. On the one hand, for example, Herman Witsius held to two primary covenants: 1) the covenant of works, and 2) the covenant of grace.[9] On the other hand, other theologians, such as Charles Hodge, organised their covenantal structure under three headings: 1) covenant of works, 2) covenant of redemption, and 3) covenant of grace.[10] Spurgeon commended both of these theologians. In his June 1863 sermon on "The Rainbow" from Genesis 9, Spurgeon noted that "Good Witsi[u]s has left us a marvellously learned and potent treatise" on the topic of covenantal theology.[11] Likewise, considering Hodge's biblical commentaries, Spurgeon commended, "The more we use Hodge, the more we value him.... With no writer do we more fully agree."[12] For Hodge, the distinguishing feature of the threefold approach was that "sometimes Christ is presented as one of the parties [of the covenant]; at others He is represented not as a party, but as the mediator and surety of the covenant; while the parties are represented to be God and his people."[13] Spurgeon noticed the same dynamic as Hodge, though he viewed the covenant of redemption as subsumed under the covenant of grace. Therefore, Spurgeon's framework followed the twofold approach: a covenant of works and a covenant of grace.

Covenant of Works

The first covenant between God and human beings was the conditional covenant of works. Spurgeon believed, "Adam was the representative man. A certain law was given him. If he kept it, he

---

9. Herman Witsius, *The Economy of the Covenants, between God and Man: Comprehending a Complete Body of Divinity* (New York: Thomas Kirk, 1798), 51.

10. See Charles Hodge, *Systematic Theology*, 3 vols. (New York: Scribner, Armstrong, and Co., 1873), 2.354–77.

11. *MTP* 9.366. The original inadvertently put an "n" in the place of the "u" in Witsius's name: "Good Witsins [*sic*]."

12. *Lectures* 4.174, 178.

13. Hodge, 2.357.

and all his posterity would be blessed as the result of obedience. If he broke it, he would incur the curse himself, and entail it on all represented by him."[14] Adam, acting as the representative head of humanity, failed to obey the law of God, and therefore failed to earn the covenantal blessings of this first covenant. In his sermon entitled "The Covenant," Spurgeon spoke of Adam's fall: "Our first covenant-head snatched greedily at the forbidden fruit, and fell.… There you, and I, and all of us, fell down."[15] By this action, it was proved to Spurgeon "once for all that by works of law no man can be justified; for if perfect Adam broke the law so readily, depend upon it, you and I would break any law that God had ever made."[16] However, the "second Adam" fulfilled this conditional covenant, and Spurgeon explained, "You know his name; he is the ever-blessed Son of the Highest."[17] Jesus Christ, by his active obedience, kept the conditional covenant of works with the Father, and secured for himself the covenantal blessings. The success of Christ was, for Spurgeon, the fulfillment of the covenant of works.

Covenant of Grace

The second covenant, in Spurgeon's framework, was the covenant of grace, which contained the eternal promise of God to bless his people. Preaching on Hebrews 13:20 in October of 1859, Spurgeon reminded his listeners at the Surrey Music Hall, "All God's dealings with men have had a covenant character."[18] Grace was the essence of that covenant, and the first parties to the everlasting covenant consisted of the three divine persons of the Godhead. Spurgeon praised:

[B]efore God had spoken existence out of nothing, before angel's wing had stirred the unnavigated ether, before a solitary song had disturbed the solemnity of the silence in which God reigned supreme, he had entered into solemn counsel with himself, with

14. *MTP* 58.517.
15. *MTP* 57.364.
16. *MTP* 57.364.
17. *MTP* 57.364.
18. *NPSP* 5.417.

his Son, and with his Spirit, and had in that council decreed, determined, purposed, and predestinated the salvation of his people.[19]

The person and work of Jesus Christ was the scope and means of fulfilling the covenant of grace. Christ was the mediator, arbiter, and surety of the covenant of grace. As Spurgeon declared, "Christ is the *sum and substance* of the covenant… although much might be said concerning the glories of the covenant, yet nothing could be said which is not to be found in that one word, 'Christ.'"[20] In Christ the covenant of works was fulfilled, and through him the eternal promises of God's covenantal blessings were distributed to his people. Recognizing that the covenant of works has been accomplished in Christ, now, according to the blessing of the eternal covenant of grace, "God on his part has solemnly pledged himself to give undeserved favour to as many as were represented in Christ Jesus."[21] Spurgeon's covenantal framework was a Trinitarian, twofold model, whereby God's people received by grace the covenantal blessings promised by the Father, to the Son, and, as the following section will prove, through the Holy Spirit.

The Spirit's Role in the Covenant of Grace

For Spurgeon, the Holy Spirit was an active participant in establishing the covenant of grace, and the one who applied to God's people the blessings promised in it. Spurgeon recognised the Spirit's participation in the covenant of grace in two particular ways: as a party in the eternal agreement and as the agent of God who applied the blessings earned by Christ. The biblical text for Spurgeon's October 2, 1859 sermon, titled "The Blood of the Everlasting Covenant," was Hebrews 13:20. Preaching on the topic of the covenant of grace, Spurgeon considered "*the high contracting parties*" with whom the covenant was first made.[22] He claimed that the eternal agreement occurred prior to the

---

19.   *NPSP* 5.419.
20.   *NPSP* 2.393.
21.   *MTP* 58.518.
22.   *NPSP* 5.418.

foundation of the world, and it was originally made "between God the Father, and God the Son; or to put it in a yet more scriptural light, it was made mutually between the three divine persons of the adorable Trinity."[23]

Spurgeon creatively depicted this intratrinitarian dialogue marking the establishment of this eternal covenant. According to Spurgeon, the Father, "the Most High Jehovah," committed to giving to his only-begotten Son a covenant people who "shall be for ever the objects of my eternal love.... these will I adopt and make my sons and daughters, and these shall reign with me through Christ eternally."[24] On the other side of the covenant, the Son committed to become man, take the form and nature of humanity, keep the law perfectly, bear the sins of God's people, be obedient unto death on the cross, rise again, ascend into heaven, intercede for God's people at the Father's right hand, and "bring all my sheep of whom, by [my] blood, thou hast constituted me the shepherd — I will bring every one safe to thee at last."[25]

In like manner, Spurgeon described that the Holy Spirit was party with the Father in their covenant with the Son. The Spirit, as Spurgeon explained, guaranteed that "all whom the Father giveth to the Son, I will in due time quicken.... I will cleanse them and drive out all depravity from them, and they shall be presented at last spotless and faultless."[26] Spurgeon outlined the Spirit's promise to "show them their need of redemption... cut off from them all groundless hope, and destroy their refuges of lies. I will bring them to the blood of sprinkling... give them faith whereby this blood shall be applied to them... work in them every grace... [and] keep their faith alive."[27] The Spirit's role in the covenant was to take the promises of the Father and the work of the Son and make them effectual to the people of God. Thus, the Spirit committed by his own volition, to come and dwell within God's people at the appointed time.

---

23. *NPSP* 5.418.

24. *NPSP* 5.419.

25. *NPSP* 5.420.

26. *NPSP* 5.419.

27. *NPSP* 5.419.

Spurgeon's favorite section of the Bible in regard to the covenant of grace was Ezekiel 36. He explained,

> Ezekiel's copy of the covenant is full and clear, and deserves to be written in letters of gold and hung up in the best chamber of every believer's dwelling. This is the *Magna Charta* of saints: the title-deed of the land of our inheritance. Glorious covenant of grace, our heart delights in every line of promise wherewith thou art enriched![28]

Among all the covenant promises of Ezekiel, Spurgeon especially highlighted the coming of God's Spirit to live within his people. Preaching on Ezekiel 36:27, Spurgeon lauded this promise of the indwelling Spirit:

> To call it a golden sentence would be much too commonplace: to liken it to a pearl of great price would be too poor a comparison. We cannot feel, much less speak, too much in praise of that great God who has put this clause into the covenant of his grace. In that covenant every sentence is more precious than heaven and earth; and this line is not the least among his choice words of promise: "I will put my spirit within you."[29]

Overall, Spurgeon preached five sermons on Ezekiel 36:27, arguing throughout that without the Holy Spirit "all things done even by the Father and by Jesus Christ would be ineffectual, for [the Holy Spirit] is needed as much as the Saviour of men, or the Father of spirits."[30] Spurgeon believed that the Holy Spirit was sent by God as a fulfillment of the intratrinitarian covenant in order to apply the covenantal blessings. The reason this covenant was characterised by grace was because the Holy Spirit applied to the Christian the blessings promised by the Father and earned by the Son—the covenant was grace all the way from promise, to fulfillment, and to the application of the blessed promises by the Holy Spirit.

---

28. *MTP* 32.517.
29. *NPSP* 37.217.
30. *MTP* 53.337.

Conclusion

Spurgeon's biblical theology was organised around a covenantal hermeneutic, and within his interpretive framework the Holy Spirit was a party of the eternal covenant and the substance of the covenant promise. He believed that the covenantal promise of God's blessing was established through the eternal, mutual, and intratrinitarian commitment of Father, Son, and Holy Spirit. While each person of the Godhead was essentially involved, as Spurgeon described, the blessings of the eternal covenant of grace were applied to God's people by the direct agency of the Holy Spirit. In this way, the Holy Spirit was, to Spurgeon, essential to the covenantal promise of salvation from eternity past all the way through the application of the promises to the Christian.

8

"The Breath of the Divine Spirit"
The Holy Spirit and Regeneration

The commencement of salvation is the Holy Spirit's work.... [M]y brethren, no man was ever saved by the means of grace apart from the Holy Spirit. You may hear the sermons of the man whom God delighteth to honour; ye may select from all your puritanical divines the writings of the man whom God did bless with a double portion of his Holy Spirit; ye may attend every meeting for prayer; ye may turn over the leaves of this blessed book; but in all this, there is no life for the soul apart from the breath of the Divine Spirit.[1]

The biblical imagery of the Holy Spirit compared to the wind captivated Spurgeon's understanding of the Spirit's work in the world. This metaphor indicated to Spurgeon that the Holy Spirit, like the wind, blows "according to his own will and pleasure amongst the sons of men."[2] In 1857, at the age of twenty-three, Spurgeon preached to the largest crowd that he would ever preach to in any building—23,654 people. He was called on to preach a fast-day sermon at the Crystal Palace to address the events of the 1857 mutiny in India, and to raise funds for the families who were directly impacted by the violence.[3]

Of the 23,000 people who heard him preach that sermon, there was one person related to that preaching event that Spurgeon never forgot about. As the place was being prepared for the

1. *NPSP* 4.107.
2. *MTP* 23.304.
3. *Autobiography* 2.239–40.

preaching event, Spurgeon arrived a couple of days early in order to test the acoustics and placement of the pulpit. In his sound check, he announced in full voice, "Behold the Lamb of God, which taketh away the sin of the world."[4] As Spurgeon explained:

> In one of the galleries, a workman, who knew nothing of what was being done, heard the words, and they came like a message from Heaven to his soul. He was smitten with conviction on account of sin, put down his tools, went home, and there, after a season of spiritual struggling, found peace and life by beholding the Lamb of God. Years after, he told this story to one who visited him on his death-bed."[5]

Spurgeon's recognition of the miraculous and unexpected way in which the Holy Spirit brought new life to that workman was a quintessential example to the preacher of the divine work of the Spirit in regeneration.

For Spurgeon, the life of the world depends on the work of the Holy Spirit, and, even more, the spiritual life of the Christian is dependent on the Spirit who, like the wind, gives life. We have already seen how instructive this biblical description of the Holy Spirit was to Spurgeon. In later chapters it will be shown again how Spurgeon relied on this metaphor. In the present chapter we will see how Spurgeon utilised this picture as the basis for explaining the Spirit's work in regeneration, which he understood as an immediate, one time, and mysterious work in which the Holy Spirit gave new life to a person who was spiritually dead. As Spurgeon understood it, regeneration was the first act of the Holy Spirit in applying redemption to the Christian. Lastly, this chapter will describe how Spurgeon saw the Spirit's work in regeneration as inherently related to the biblical theme of adoption.

The Spirit Like the Wind

Spurgeon found it remarkable that in both biblical Hebrew and Greek, the word for "spirit" was the same word for "wind" or

---

4. *Autobiography* 2.239.
5. *Autobiography* 2.239.

"breath."[6] He called attention to this fact on numerous occasions in his preaching. In one of these sermons, he explained, "Wind is, of all material things, one of the most spiritual in appearance; it is invisible, ethereal, mysterious; hence, men have fixed upon it as being nearest akin to spirit."[7]

Translating the Greek word πνεῦμα (*pneuma*) as "breath" was also insightful to explain the Spirit's work in regeneration. The Holy Spirit is the divine breath of God who breathed life into human beings at creation and now spiritually regenerates the Christian to new life. When Spurgeon preached on this use of the metaphor, he often quoted Isaac Watts's hymn "Regeneration": "The Spirit, like some heavenly wind, // Blows on the sons of flesh, // Inspires us with a heavenly mind, // And forms the man afresh."[8] The Holy Spirit, like the wind, regenerates a Christian by breathing new life into that person.

Spurgeon believed that without the regenerating work of the Holy Spirit there is no hope for new life. There is no ability within any person to create this new birth for oneself. Prior to the Spirit's work in this way every person is spiritually dead. As Spurgeon conveyed in his sermon on "The Spirit's work in the New Creation":

> There is not a hand there to be lifted, nor even an ear to hear, nor an eye to see, nor a pulse that can beat. We do not exaggerate nor go beyond the truth when we say this; and every man is thus dead till the Spirit of God comes to him; and when the Spirit comes to him, he finds nothing in him that can co-operate with the Spirit of God, but everything that is to be good must be created in him, and be brought to him, and be infused into him.[9]

---

6. The Hebrew term Spurgeon referred to was רוּחַ, meaning "breath, wind, spirit" [Francis Brown, S. R. Driver, and C. A. Briggs, *The Brown-Driver-Briggs Hebrew and English Lexicon* (Peabody: Hendrickson Publishers, 1981), 924]. The Greek term was πνεῦμα, meaning wind, breath, life, soul, and spirit [Hermann Kleinknecht, "πνεῦμα," *Theological Dictionary of the New Testament* (Grand Rapids: Wm. B. Eerdmans Publishing Company, 1964–1976), 6.332–59].

7. *MTP* 27.522.

8. *NPSP* 4.18. See Isaac Watts, *An Arrangement of the Psalms, Hymns, and Spiritual Songs of the Rev. Isaac Watts*, ed. James M. Winchell (Boston: Gould and Lincoln, 1832), 219.

9. *MTP* 55.111.

He summarised with a vivid word picture: "Man's nature is a charnel-house, and a sepulchre, and a little hell; and God's Spirit must bring to it that which is living, and good, and pleasing in God's sight if it is ever to be there."[10] As Spurgeon's preaching popularity grew, he remained committed to communicating that only the Holy Spirit is able to bring new life to a person. Less than a month after preaching to those 23,654 people at the Crystal Palace, and knowing that more people than ever before were hearing his preaching, Spurgeon exhorted his listeners to recognise that "there is no life for the soul apart from the breath of the Divine Spirit."[11] While regeneration may be "mimicked," or a person "pretend to be regenerated," without the Holy Spirit's work a person cannot receive new life.[12]

For Spurgeon, regeneration was a "supremely supernatural" and mysterious act.[13] He defined regeneration as the primary and essential work of the Holy Spirit in the process of salvation. Without the work of regeneration, no other spiritual blessing is possible. In his sermon titled "The Teaching of the Holy Ghost," Spurgeon explained that the Holy Spirit applies "all the privileges of the new covenant, beginning from regeneration, running through redemption, justification, pardon, sanctification, adoption, preservation, continual safety, even unto an abundant entrance into the kingdom of our Lord and Saviour Jesus Christ."[14] Until the Spirit regenerates the Christian, none of the other privileges of the new covenant can be applied.

Moreover, for Spurgeon, the Spirit's work in regeneration was mysterious. In his May 3, 1857 sermon titled "Regeneration," Spurgeon admitted the perception that his theology of regeneration "is called fanatical doctrine."[15] Yet he would not back away from his commitment to the utter necessity of the Spirit to give new life, even as mysterious as this work proved to be. In that May

---

10.   *MTP* 55.111.
11.   *NPSP* 4.107.
12.   *NPSP* 4.18.
13.   *NPSP* 4.18.
14.   *NPSP* 6.232.
15.   *NPSP* 3.188.

1857 sermon, he declared, "There must be a divine operation, call it a miraculous operation, if you please.... There must be a divine interposition, a divine working, a divine influence, or else do what you may, without that you perish, and are undone."[16] Preaching on the same topic seventeen years later, Spurgeon again affirmed the mysterious nature of the Spirit's work in regeneration. While he could not "explain the mystery of the new birth," he believed "new birth is a great necessity."[17] The only explanation he could provide was that regeneration is "the work of God the Holy Spirit; the new birth, a thing that is from above."[18] Only by the Holy Spirit's divine action, mysterious as it may be, could a person be born again in Jesus Christ.

Lastly, as Spurgeon depicted, regeneration and biblical adoption were works that the Holy Spirit accomplished, and the two were inherently related. In his sermon on January 7, 1877, he explained that with regeneration, as in new birth, Christians receive from the Holy Spirit "the nature of children."[19] He understood Galatians 4:6 in this light — "because ye are sons, God hath sent forth the Spirit of his Son into your hearts, crying, Abba, Father." Spurgeon introduced his September 22, 1878 sermon with a Trinitarian description of the Christian's adoption, explaining that the Holy Spirit brings the Christian into "sweet communion with the Father through his Son Jesus Christ, to his glory and to our benefit."[20] Then, using nearly identical language from his January 7, 1877 sermon, he described, "Adoption gives us the rights of children, regeneration gives us the nature of children."[21] This language was worth repeating because it captured the related, though distinctive, features of the biblical ideas of regeneration and adoption. It was also helpful language to repeat because it allowed Spurgeon to explain the Spirit's essential role in both

---

16. *NPSP* 3.188.
17. *MTP* 54.578.
18. *NPSP* 4.107.
19. *MTP* 23.19.
20. *MTP* 24.530.
21. *MTP* 24.530.

regeneration and adoption, as it applied to the Christian. The Holy Spirit, as the Spirit of the Son, "puts the cry [of sonship] into the heart and mouth of the believer.... [the Holy Spirit] suggests it, approves of it, and educates us to it. We should never have cried thus if [the Holy Spirit] had not first taught us the way."[22] The Spirit's work in regeneration provides the basis for the Christian to then call out to God as Father. Adoption, then, *comes to us by redemption*" (emphasis added) so that "Sonship [is] sealed by the indwelling Spirit."[23] For Spurgeon, regeneration was a work of new birth accomplished by the Holy Spirit, which was then the basis for the Spirit's work in affirming and completing the adoption of the Christian into the family of God.

Conclusion

In his May 27, 1877 sermon on John 3:8, Spurgeon summarised the need and nature of his theology of regeneration by explaining, "Two great truths are written in letters of light over the gate of heaven, as the requisites of all who enter there—*Reconciliation by the blood of Jesus Christ*; and *Regeneration by the work of the Holy Ghost*."[24] Spurgeon believed that regeneration was a supernatural operation of the Holy Spirit, whereby he applied to the Christian the redemption earned in Jesus Christ. Without the work of Jesus Christ, reconciliation with God would not be possible. Likewise, without the work of the Holy Spirit, the work of Christ would be ineffectual for the Christian. Therefore, the Holy Spirit, like the wind, gives new life to Christians, and secures for them the status and nature of children of God. Spurgeon affirmed that without the regenerating work of the Holy Spirit none of the other spiritual blessings were possible.

---

22. *MTP* 24.537.
23. *MTP* 24.532, 536.
24. *MTP* 23.302 (emphasis added).

9

"The Spirit of Truth"
The Holy Spirit and Conversion

This person is "he, the Spirit," the "Spirit of truth;" not an influence or an emanation, but actually a person. "When the Spirit of truth is come, he shall guide you into all truth."... I remember sitting one day in the house of God and hearing a sermon as dry as possible, and as worthless as all such sermons are, when a thought struck my mind—how came I to be converted? I prayed, thought I. Then I thought how came I to pray? I was induced to pray by reading the Scriptures. How came I to read the Scriptures? Why—I did read them; and what led me to that? And then, in a moment, I saw that God was at the bottom of all, and that he was the author of faith. And then the whole doctrine opened up to me, from which I have not departed.[1]

There is no one who can tell the story of Spurgeon's conversion better than Spurgeon himself. This excerpt from his *Autobiography* captures the details of his own conversion experience which took place in January 1850:

I sometimes think I might have been in darkness and despair until now had it not been for the goodness of God in sending a snowstorm, one Sunday morning, while I was going to a certain place of worship. When I could go no further, I turned down a side street, and came to a little Primitive Methodist Chapel. In that chapel there may have been a dozen or fifteen people. I had heard of the Primitive Methodists, how they sang so loudly that they made people's heads ache; but that did not matter to

1. *NPSP* 1.383–84.

me. I wanted to know how I might be saved, and if they could tell me that, I did not care how much they made my head ache. The minister did not come that morning; he was snowed up, I suppose. At last, a very thin-looking man, a shoemaker, or tailor, or something of that sort, went up into the pulpit to preach. Now, it is well that preachers should be instructed; but this man was really stupid. He was obliged to stick to his text, for the simple reason that he had little else to say. The text was, — "LOOK UNTO ME, AND BE YE SAVED, ALL THE ENDS OF THE EARTH."

He did not even pronounce the words rightly, but that did not matter. There was, I thought, a glimpse of hope for me in that text. The preacher began thus: — "My dear friends, this is a very simple text indeed. It says, 'Look.' Now lookin' don't take a deal of pains. It ain't liftin' your foot or your finger; it is just, 'Look.' Well, a man needn't go to College to learn to look. You may be the biggest fool, and yet you can look. A man needn't be worth a thousand a year to be able to look. Anyone can look; even a child can look. But then the text says, 'Look unto *Me*.' Ay!" said he, in broad Essex, "many [of] ye are lookin' to yourselves, but it's no use lookin' there. You'll never find any comfort in yourselves. Some look to God the Father. No, look to Him by-and-by. Jesus Christ says, 'Look unto *Me*.' Some of ye say, 'We must wait for the Spirit's workin'.' You have no business with that just now. Look to *Christ*. The text says, 'Look unto *Me*.'"

Then the good man followed up his text in this way: — "Look unto Me; I am sweatin' great drops of blood. Look unto Me; I am hangin' on the cross. Look unto Me; I am dead and buried. Look unto Me; I rise again. Look unto Me; I ascend to Heaven. Look unto Me; I am sittin' at the Father's right hand. O poor sinner, look unto Me! look unto Me!"

When he had gone to about that length, and managed to spin out ten minutes or so, he was at the end of his tether. Then he looked at me under the gallery, and I daresay, with so few present, he knew me to be a stranger. Just fixing his eyes on me, as if he knew all my heart, he said, "Young man, you look very miserable." Well, I did; but I had not been accustomed to have remarks made from the pulpit on my personal appearance before. However, it was a good blow, struck right home. He continued, "and you always will be miserable — miserable in life, and miserable in death, —

if you don't obey my text; but if you obey now, this moment, you will be saved." Then, lifting up his hands, he shouted, as only a Primitive Methodist could do, "Young man, look to Jesus Christ. Look! Look! Look! You have nothin' to do but to look and live." I saw at once the way of salvation. I know not what else he said, — I did not take much notice of it, — I was so possessed with that one thought. Like as when the brazen serpent was lifted up, the people only looked and were healed, so it was with me. I had been waiting to do fifty things, but when I heard that word, "Look!" what a charming word it seemed to me! Oh! I looked until I could almost have looked my eyes away. There and then the cloud was gone, the darkness had rolled away, and that moment I saw the sun; and I could have risen that instant, and sung with the most enthusiastic of them, of the precious blood of Christ, and the simple faith which looks alone to Him.[2]

The four key themes of Spurgeon's conversion, which he highlighted in his own account of it, were the sovereignty of God, the preceding work of the Holy Spirit, the Holy Spirit's work at the time of conversion, and the Christ-centred nature of conversion. First, Spurgeon maintained the sovereignty of God for his conversion. He marvelled at the details that led him to enter that place of worship on that Sunday morning. As he recounted, "I sometimes think I might have been in darkness and despair until now had it not been for the goodness of God in sending a snow storm, one Sunday morning, while I was going to a certain place of worship."[3] Six years later, Spurgeon preached on

---

2. *Autobiography* 1.105–06. For Spurgeon's full account of his conversion, see *Autobiography* 1.97–115. For a discussion of the date and preacher of the "Look" sermon, see Timothy Albert McCoy, "The Evangelistic Ministry of C. H. Spurgeon: Implications for a Contemporary Model for Pastoral Evangelism" PhD Dissertation, The Southern Baptist Theological Seminary, 1989, 323–50. There is disagreement among historians about the identity of the preacher of the "Look" sermon, and whether the date of the sermon was January 6, 1850 or January 13, 1850. I agree with McCoy that Robert Eaglen was most likely the preacher of that sermon. Moreover, I find that the evidence in favor of January 13, 1850 presents a formidable argument as the actual date of Spurgeon's conversion, which is contrary to what Spurgeon himself recorded. Particularly relevant for the January 13 date is the handbook schedule for Eaglen's preaching rotation, and the weather service records of snow on January 12, 1850 (Ibid., 349–50). However, Spurgeon himself recorded and defended the date of January 6, 1850, and his early affirmation and firsthand testimony is difficult to refute.

3. *Autobiography* 1.105.

Isaiah 45:22, the sermon text from his conversion experience. His description of how God works in conversion was overt by the title of his sermon, "Sovereignty and Salvation."[4] Spurgeon believed that conversion was a sovereign work of God.

Second, Spurgeon believed that the Holy Spirit had been at work prior to his conversion to prepare him for that moment. Spurgeon expressed that in the time leading up to his conversion experience, he was convicted of his own sin and desiring forgiveness. He described, "When I was in the hand of the Holy Spirit, under conviction of sin, I had a clear and sharp sense of the justice of God."[5] He attended all of the churches in his city because he "desired to know how a poor sinner, under a sense of sin, might find peace with God.... I was like a dog under the table not allowed to eat the children's food."[6] His own testimony revealed that without the prior and direct work of the Holy Spirit, Spurgeon would not have had his conversion experience. As such, Spurgeon understood that a Christian's conversion was preceded by the work of the Holy Spirit in regeneration and conviction of sin.

Third, Spurgeon believed that the Holy Spirit was the direct agent of his conversion at the moment it occurred. Again, reflecting on his conversion experience and retracing the steps that led to the very moment of conversion, he recognised, "And then, in a moment, I saw that God was at the bottom of all, and that he was the author of faith."[7] Spurgeon had grown up with Christian parents and grandparents who all taught him about Jesus. As a child, he had been "cradled by prayerful hands, and lulled to sleep by songs concerning Jesus."[8] For his whole life prior to January 1850, Spurgeon regularly heard the gospel. However, as he described, in that moment "the power of the Holy Spirit was present to open my ear, and to guide the message to my heart."[9]

---

4. *NPSP* 2, sermon 60.

5. *Autobiography* 1.98.

6. *Autobiography* 1.105.

7. *NPSP* 1.384.

8. *Autobiography* 1.102.

9. *Autobiography* 1.102.

By the work of the Holy Spirit, Spurgeon's mind was enlightened to the gospel and his heart was struck with its truth.

Fourth, Spurgeon's conversion was centred on Jesus Christ. As Spurgeon searched for salvation, the preacher that morning looked at him and said, "Young man, look to Jesus Christ. Look! Look! Look! You have nothin' to do but look and live."[10] At these words, the young Spurgeon "saw at once the way of salvation."[11] The word "look" conveyed that the work of salvation was accomplished by Jesus Christ and not by the one receiving the salvation. At the same time, Spurgeon believed it was the Holy Spirit who enabled the Christian to look to Christ. Therefore, as Spurgeon described, all the meaning of his conversion experience was wrapped up in that one word, "'Look, look, look!'—Four letters, and two of them alike!… Some divines want a week to tell you what you are to do to be saved: but God the Holy Ghost only wants four letters to do it."[12] As with Spurgeon's own testimony, even a person's ability to look to Jesus Christ for salvation was empowered by the Holy Spirit. These four themes identified in Spurgeon's conversion laid the groundwork for his theology of the Spirit's work in conversion.

Having established in the previous chapter Spurgeon's belief that regeneration was a work of the Holy Spirit in the life of a Christian, in this chapter, we will see that Spurgeon believed that conversion was also fully dependent on the Holy Spirit. While Spurgeon ascribed regeneration and conversion as early and related works of the Spirit in the life of a Christian, he was clear in distinguishing them as separate operations of the Holy Spirit. Moreover, as we will see in this chapter, the themes of Spurgeon's own conversion experience proved instructive as he later developed a biblical theology of conversion and the essential work of the Spirit in it.

Regeneration and Conversion

10. *Autobiography* 1.106.

11. *Autobiography* 1.106.

12. *NPSP* 2.54–55.

When describing Spurgeon's theology of salvation, one must be careful not to confuse his theology of conversion with his theology of regeneration since Spurgeon himself distinguished regeneration and conversion as two separate operations of the Holy Spirit. Spurgeon understood conversion as the work of the Holy Spirit in which, after regeneration, the Spirit enlivens the Christian's heart, will, and imagination to the truths of God. Like regeneration, Spurgeon believed that conversion was fully dependent on the Holy Spirit. At the same time, Spurgeon recognised regeneration and conversion as separate operations of the Holy Spirit. After demonstrating Spurgeon's view on the distinct natures of regeneration and conversion, it will be shown how Spurgeon's own conversion shaped his theological position on the topic, followed by Spurgeon's understanding of the Spirit's direct role in the conversion of a Christian.

Admittedly, Spurgeon was not immune to incidentally blurring the distinction between regeneration and conversion. For example, preaching at Surrey Music Hall in the summer of 1858, he was discussing the mysterious nature of the new birth when he stated, "I take it that the Holy Spirit's work in conversion is two-fold. First, it is an awakening of the powers that man already has, and secondly, it is an implantation of powers which he never had at all."[13] Commenting on the first point, he explained, "In the great work of the new birth, the Holy Spirit first of all *awakens the mental powers*."[14] That explanation of what the Spirit does in the work of new birth is best identified under Spurgeon's understanding of regeneration, as the previous chapter has shown. So, to describe this as the first of the twofold work of conversion is to potentially confuse the distinction he intended to make between regeneration and conversion.

In other places, Spurgeon was clearer on his understanding of this distinction, and the importance for maintaining it. In his November 5, 1857 sermon on "The Work of the Holy Spirit," Spurgeon argued, "We must always learn to distinguish between

---

13. *NPSP* 4.291.
14. *NPSP* 4.291 (emphasis added).

regeneration and conversion."[15] In sequencing the work of the Holy Spirit in the Christian, Spurgeon believed regeneration occurred first and conversion followed. As he argued, "Conversion is a thing which is caused by regeneration, but regeneration is the very first act of God the Spirit in the soul."[16] Likewise, thirty-one years later Spurgeon argued that conversion "is the first apparent result of regeneration, or the new birth."[17] Again, in an 1874 sermon where he was answering the question "Is Conversion Necessary?" Spurgeon explained, "Regeneration and conversion, the one the secret cause, and the other the first overt effect, produce a great change in the character."[18] It was important to maintain the distinction between regeneration and conversion since, as Spurgeon believed, regeneration was a one-time occurrence in a Christian, while conversion might occur multiple times in a Christian's life. Moreover, regeneration occurred mysteriously, while conversion was a conscious experience for the Christian. Once a Christian has received new birth, then it is not possible to receive it a second time. However, the Christian, in his or her life, might find that the Holy Spirit provides conscious moments of supernatural clarity that feel to the Christian that an awakening has occurred—which would be, as Spurgeon described, a conversion experience. In this way, Spurgeon was careful to set apart conversion as a unique operation of the Holy Spirit in the life of the Christian.

The Spirit like Cleansing Water

If the Spirit's work in regeneration was best depicted as the Spirit working like the wind, in conversion Spurgeon utilised the biblical imagery of the Holy Spirit operating like cleansing water. He drew this imagery of the Spirit working like water from John 3:5, where "We are told that we are 'born-again of water and of the Spirit.'"[19] When the Spirit converts a Christian, he purifies

---

15. *NPSP* 4.108.
16. *NPSP* 4.108.
17. *MTP* 35.494.
18. *MTP* 20.401.
19. *NPSP* 4.21.

the soul and cleanses the heart so that no converted Christian "is to-day as foul a liver as he was before his pretended conversion."[20] In conversion, "the Holy Spirit when he comes in the heart comes like water."[21]

In what ways does the Spirit cleanse the Christian? Spurgeon's theology of conversion was based on the biblical themes evident in his own conversion experience—namely, the sovereignty of God, the preceding work of the Holy Spirit, the Holy Spirit's work at the time of the conversion, and the Christ-centred nature of conversion. Spurgeon added to these descriptions three ways in which the Spirit cleanses the Christian in conversion. In his 1855 sermon entitled "The Power of the Holy Spirit" Spurgeon articulated the threefold operation of the Holy Spirit: 1) on the heart, 2) on the will, and 3) on the imagination. In conversion, the Spirit, like cleansing water, washes the Christian, transforming the heart, will, and imagination.

First, the work of the Spirit in conversion was to turn the heart of a Christian. Certainly, there was a way in which this heart change required the enlightening of the mind. For Spurgeon, if a person is to see one's own sin, or see Jesus for who he truly is, then that person "must have been quickened and made alive; otherwise he could not be capable of feeling, or seeing, or discerning at all."[22] Thus, in conversion, the Holy Spirit enlightens the mind and gives understanding regarding the truth of Jesus Christ. Nevertheless, Spurgeon believed that the conversion of the Christian's heart, whereby one turns from a love for sin to a love for Christ, was a greater change than that of the mind. In this way, repentance was a necessary part of conversion. Preaching in April 1868 on Acts 3:19, Spurgeon explained, "Conversion, if translated, means a turning round, a turning from, and a turning to—a turning from sin, a turning to holiness—a turning from carelessness to thought, from the world to heaven, from self to Jesus—a complete turning."[23] The Spirit, according to Spurgeon, is the only one who

---

20. *NPSP* 4.21.

21. *NPSP* 4.21.

22. *NPSP* 4.109.

23. *MTP* 14.195.

can turn a person in such a way because "The Spirit alone has power over man's heart."[24] Thus Spurgeon understood that the Holy Spirit alone rules over the heart and empowers the turning of the Christian's heart in conversion.

Second, the Holy Spirit also operated in the Christian to convert his or her will to align with the will of God. Spurgeon asserted, "If there is one thing more stubborn than the heart it is *the will*."[25] Whereas the conversion of the heart was about loving the right things, the conversion of the will was about wanting to love the right things. Spurgeon believed that free will existed prior to the fall of humans, and that the free will of the first human beings created a "terrible mess."[26] After that fall, the will of human beings always leads to sin, but "the Holy Spirit has power over the will."[27] Though the human will leads to sin the Holy Spirit can change the will of a person so that he or she will desire to please God. Spurgeon explained that the Holy Spirit miraculously "maketh the unwilling sinner so willing that he is impetuous after the gospel; he who was obstinate, now hurries to the cross."[28] As Spurgeon described, even the "will to be converted is in great part conversion," which is also a work that "God the Holy Spirit must begin."[29] In conversion, the Holy Spirit changes the will of a Christian so that he or she longs for life in Jesus Christ.

Third, Spurgeon described the Spirit's work in conversion as a renewal of the imagination. He depicted the converting work of the Holy Spirit in ascending levels: "The will is somewhat worse than the heart to bend, but there is one thing that excels the will in its naughtiness, and that is the *imagination*."[30] If a Christian's imagination remained unconverted, then through its sinfulness a person would continue to grieve the Holy Spirit, which was

---

24. *NPSP* 1.233.
25. *NPSP* 1.234 (emphasis added).
26. *NPSP* 1.234.
27. *NPSP* 1.234.
28. *NPSP* 1.234.
29. *NPSP* 4.108.
30. *NPSP* 1.234.

Spurgeon's greatest fear as a Christian. He believed, "If you indulge in lascivious expressions, or if even you allow imagination to doat upon any lascivious act, or if your heart goes after covetousness, if you set your heart upon anything that is evil, the Spirit of God will be grieved."[31] No person is able to restrain wandering and evil thoughts, nor manage one's own "filthy lusts."[32] Spurgeon felt that these temptations were particularly challenging for him since he had such an active imagination. He was prone to sin against the Holy Spirit in this way, yet he believed that the Spirit could restrain the imagination of a person. Spurgeon asked and answered, "Can you contain your imagination? No; but the power of the Holy Ghost can."[33] In conversion, the Spirit constrains the Christian's imagination to prevent the Christian from harboring sinful thoughts and grieving the Holy Spirit.

Conclusion

Spurgeon understood that conversion was a distinct operation of the Holy Spirit, following regeneration, and included a turning of a Christian away from sin and toward the things of God. The only hope for a person to be enlightened to the truth of Christ is for the Holy Spirit to give insight and understanding. A person might spend time "hearing, reading, and thinking" about the Scriptures "and yet never discern the Lord's Christ."[34] Therefore, as Spurgeon held, there is an "*absolute necessity of the Holy Spirit's influence*, if we could see men converted."[35] Moreover, Spurgeon's theology of conversion was instructed by his own conversion experience, which he recognised as the biblical description of conversion. He taught that conversion was God's sovereign work, that conversion required the preceding work of the Holy Spirit in the life of a person, that the special work of the Spirit was necessary at the moment of conversion, and that conversion accomplished by the Spirit was centred around Jesus Christ. More

---

31. *NPSP* 5.430.
32. *NPSP* 5.430.
33. *NPSP* 1.234.
34. *MTP* 34.487.
35. *NPSP* 4.291 (emphasis added).

specifically, Spurgeon believed that in conversion the Holy Spirit washes over the Christian like water in order to change the heart, will, and imagination of the Christian. As the Holy Spirit is the Spirit of truth, therefore without the Spirit's divine, direct, and personal agency true conversion is impossible.

10

"The Sanctifier"
The Holy Spirit and Sanctification

Holiness is not mere morality, not the outward keeping of divine precepts out of a hard sense of duty, while those commandments in themselves are not delightful to us. Holiness is the entirety of our manhood fully consecrated to the Lord and moulded to his will. This is the thing which the church of God must have, but it can never have it apart from the Sanctifier, for there is not a grain of holiness beneath the sky but what is of the operation of the Holy Ghost.[1]

Chief among Spurgeon's reading interests was biblical theology. In order to approximate the amount of theological reading that Spurgeon completed during his pastorate in London, his wife explained, "It would be necessary to make a list of nearly all the principal theological and biographical works published during that period, and to add to it a large portion of the other standard literature of the present and previous centuries, and almost the whole of the volumes issued by the great divines of the Puritan period."[2] Even with so extensive a background in theological readings, Spurgeon was cautious, even reticent, to utilise theological language or quotations in his books or sermons. He wanted to avoid any deterrence that might prevent a common person from hearing and understanding the gospel. Susannah,

---

1. *MTP* 23.20.
2. *Autobiography* 4.304.

again, sheds light on this topic when she describes her husband's preaching:

> Perhaps there is a very learned man sitting over yonder, and the temptation to the preacher to say something that shall make him feel that the minister to whom he is listening is not so ignorant as some people suppose; but if there is an unlearned, simple sinner anywhere in the place, the preacher's business is just to chop his words down to that poor man's condition, and let the learned hearer receive the same message if he will.[3]

Spurgeon himself conveyed the same approach during a Sunday evening sermon:

> The preacher must also mind that he preaches Christ *very simply*. He must break up his big words and long sentences, and pray against the temptation to use them. It is usually the short, dagger-like sentence that does the work best. A true servant of Christ must never try to let the people see how well he can preach; he must never go out of his way to drag a pretty piece of poetry in his sermon, nor to introduce some fine quotations from the classics. He must employ a simple, homely style, or such a style as God has given him; and he must preach Christ so plainly that his hearers can not only understand him, but that they cannot misunderstand him even if they try to do so.[4]

A prime example of Spurgeon's ability to engage with complex theological matter and communicate its truth in common language was in his teaching on the doctrine of sanctification.

Firstly, Spurgeon described sanctification by differentiating it from justification. He explained, "There are two kinds of perfection which a Christian needs—one is the perfection of justification in the person of Jesus; and the other is, the perfection of sanctification worked in him by the Holy Spirit."[5] While the work of Jesus was completed, the work of the Spirit continues, since "At present corruption still rests even in the breasts of the regenerate. At present the heart is partially impure. At

---

3. *Autobiography* 4.268.

4. *MTP* 56.489.

5. *NPSP* 1.235.

present there are still lusts and evil imaginations."[6] Therefore, as Spurgeon understood, the Christian is holy in Christ, but he or she must also be perfected in holiness by the Holy Spirit. In other words, the work of sanctification was the Holy Spirit's application of the completed work of Christ. Spurgeon argued, "Sanctification is a work *in* us, not a work *for* us. It is a work in us, and there are two agents: one is the worker who works this sanctification effectually—that is the Spirit: and the other, the agent, the efficacious means by which the Spirit works this sanctification is—Jesus Christ and his most precious blood."[7] For Spurgeon, justification in Christ and sanctification by the Spirit were distinct, though interrelated, operations.

Secondly, Spurgeon recognised that the term sanctification referred both to the broad process of salvation (including regeneration, conversion, and perseverance, for example), and to a particular work of the Spirit within this process of salvation. For instance, Spurgeon's aim in his February 9, 1862 sermon was to teach on the "doctrine of sanctification," and he "intended to use the word 'sanctification' in the mode in which it is understood among theologians; for you must know that the term 'sanctification' has a far narrower meaning in bodies of divinity than it has in Scripture."[8] However, as he studied the topic of sanctification in Scripture, he became "lost in its ever widening extent."[9] Therefore, he divided the sermon into three biblical uses of the concept of sanctification, which he labelled 1) set apart, 2) declared as holy, and 3) made holy. It was the third meaning that Spurgeon equated with the particular definition of sanctification in which the Spirit works *actually to purify or make holy* the Christian.[10] In this particular definition of sanctification, the Christian is called to "strive after practical holiness," and in this way, Spurgeon understood sanctification to refer to a separate and

---

6. *NPSP* 1.235.
7. *MTP* 8.93.
8. *MTP* 8.86.
9. *MTP* 8.86.
10. *MTP* 8.92.

essential operation of the Holy Spirit toward the Christian within the overall process of salvation.[11]

The Holy Spirit's Work in Sanctification

Spurgeon believed that the Spirit's work in the life of a Christian was not only to bring them to salvation but also to transform the Christian so that he or she would turn from sinful behavior and live more like Jesus. One prime example of this transformation that Spurgeon urged for throughout his ministry was, for example, a Christian's approach to the use of alcoholic beverages. In his childhood, Spurgeon once heard his grandfather talking about a man named Roads, who was a member of the church his grandfather pastored. Mr. Roads "was in the habit of frequenting the public-house to have his 'drop of beer', and smoke his pipe, greatly to the grief of his godly pastor, who often heaved a sigh at the thought of his unhappy member's inconsistent conduct."[12] So, the boy Spurgeon walked down to the pub and, finding "Old Roads" with his pipe and mug of beer, walked up to the man, pointed his finger at him, and declared, "What doest thou here, Elijah? sitting with the ungodly; and you a member of a church, and breaking your pastor's heart. I'm ashamed of you! I wouldn't break my pastor's heart, I'm sure."[13] The grown man was so convicted by the boy's words that he put down his pipe, left his mug, and found a lonely spot to repent of his sin and ask the Lord for forgiveness. Then, the man went directly to his pastor's home, asked the pastor for forgiveness, and committed to "never grieve you any more, my dear pastor."[14]

Whether or not this childhood event was a catalyst for which Spurgeon set his mind against the abuse of alcohol, this topic was a consistent and grave concern throughout his ministry. Spurgeon produced two volumes of books called *John Ploughman's Talks* and *John Ploughman's Pictures* where the goal was to write books of godly wisdom in plain language. In the preface to the second

---

11. *MTP* 8.96.
12. *Autobiography* 1.23.
13. *Autobiography* 1.24.
14. *Autobiography* 1.24.

book, he contended, "To smite evil—and especially that monster evil of drink—has been my earnest endeavor, and assuredly there is need."[15] Spurgeon certainly believed that those who were caught in worldly sin could be saved out of it: "What! Did Christ shed his blood for thieves, and harlots, and drunkards? Yes, sir! as much as for the self-righteous, and even more so, for while the self-righteous miss of heaven by reason of their pride and refusal of his salvation, some of these, coming humbly to the Cross, find pardon through the precious blood."[16] Nevertheless, the "vice of drunkenness" was "sufficiently rampant to cause sorrow in every Christian bosom."[17]

This particular vice provided a clear example that in Spurgeon's ministry he understood the biblical call for a Christian to continuously grow in becoming sanctified in every area of life. This process was an operation done by the Holy Spirit in the life of a Christian. As Spurgeon described it, there were three key elements of the Spirit's work in sanctification: 1) convicting the Christian of sin, 2) causing the Christian to live a godly life, and 3) perfecting holiness in the Christian. In these ways, the Holy Spirit accomplishes his aim to make the Christian holy.

Conviction

Spurgeon believed that conviction, the Holy Spirit's foremost work in sanctification, was painful, leads to joy, and prefigured final judgement. In order to eradicate sin, the Spirit's primary work of conviction was painful to the Christian. The biblical metaphor that Spurgeon used to describe the Spirit's work in sanctification was the Spirit compared to fire. In his December 13, 1857 sermon, Spurgeon conveyed, "After the Spirit, like the wind, has made the dead sinner live, then comes the Spirit like fire."[18] While fire "has a searching and tormenting power," it also purifies, though "it purifies by a terrible process."[19] This image depicted that the Holy

15. *Pictures* 3.
16. *MTP* 59.88.
17. *Pictures* 3.
18. *NPSP* 4.19.
19. *NPSP* 4.19.

Spirit, after giving new life, lights a fire in the Christian's heart to begin burning away sin, which often proves to be spiritually painful to the Christian.

In his own experience with the Spirit's conviction of sin, Spurgeon related, "A stirring began in my heart, and I began to feel that in the sight of God I was a lost, ruined, and condemned sinner. That conviction I could not shake off."[20] In his later teaching, he described the Spirit's conviction of sin as "an awful lesson indeed to learn; and when the Holy Spirit makes us sit down upon the stool of penitence, and begins to drill this great truth into us, that sin is damnation in the bud, that it is hell in the germ: then when we begin to perceive it, we cry out, 'Now I know how vile I am; my soul abhorreth itself in dust and ashes.'"[21] Spurgeon referred to this process as "The Withering Work of the Spirit," whereby "There must be brought home to us the sentence of death upon our former legal and carnal life... *this withering work in the soul is very painful.*"[22]

At the same time, Spurgeon acknowledged that the bitterness of the Spirit's conviction will lead to joy for the Christian. Preaching on Galatians 5:22 on February 6, 1881, Spurgeon described, "When we look to Christ by the work of the Spirit one of the first fruits is sorrow.... But this sorrow is not the ultimate object of the Spirit's work, it is a means to an end."[23] The purpose of the Spirit's conviction of sin is to bring joy in Jesus Christ. The Spirit works in the Christian to bring death to the flesh so that the "incorruptible seed of the word of God, implanted by the Holy Ghost, may be in us, and abide in us for ever."[24] Therefore, Spurgeon exhorted his listeners who were experiencing the conviction of the Holy Spirit, "Rejoice, dear brother, however low you are brought, for if the Spirit humbles you he means no evil, but he intends infinite good to your soul!"[25] Spurgeon, as a seasoned pastor, held out hope to

20. *NPSP* 4.19.
21. *NPSP* 6.231.
22. *MTP* 17.375, 381.
23. *MTP* 27.73–74.
24. *MTP* 17.375.
25. *MTP* 17.382.

those under the withering conviction of sin, and turned their attention to the good that comes with the Spirit's sanctification: "O my brethren, look well to it that ye bring forth the genuine, holy, sacred, delicious fruit of the Spirit, which in one of its forms is 'joy.' Do not covet the counterfeit of earthly joy, but seek to the good Spirit to bear the true fruit in you."[26] The Holy Spirit, through painful conviction of sin, ultimately brings the gift of joy to the Christian.

Spurgeon also believed that the Holy Spirit's present work of conviction prefigured the Spirit's work at the final judgement. On February 25, 1883, Spurgeon preached a sermon titled "The Holy Spirit's Threefold Conviction of Men," based on John 16:8–11. Spurgeon understood that text of Scripture as "a compendium of all the work of the Spirit of God."[27] As an outline to the sermon, Spurgeon used three different English words to unpack the single Greek verb ἐλέγχω—reprove, convince, and convict.[28] Reproving referred to the initial and painful work of sanctification and convincing referred to conversion. When Spurgeon used the term "convict" in this sermon he meant the present conviction of the Spirit, as described above, but he especially described it as the conviction of the Spirit at final judgement. Just as the Spirit presently convicts the world of the truth of Jesus Christ, so too, Spurgeon believed, the Holy Spirit "shall make men see the judgment. Before the day actually comes, they shall perceive that since Christ has judged the devil... assuredly he will smite all that are in the dominion of Satan, and will not allow one of them to escape."[29] Considering the Spirit's work in final judgement, Spurgeon then described, "The cause of evil is judged, and its case is desperate. Oh, how the Spirit of God will convict men at that last day when they hear the Judge say, 'Come, ye blessed

---

26. *MTP* 27.75.

27. *MTP* 29.122.

28. The Greek term Spurgeon referenced was ἐλέγξει, which is a cognate of the term ἐλέγχω, with a range of meaning including to blame, reprove, convince, reveal, expose, set right, and show someone his sin and summon him to repentance [Friedrich Büchsel, "ἐλέγχω," *Theological Dictionary of the New Testament* (Grand Rapids: Wm. B. Eerdmans Publishing Company, 1964–1976), 2.473–76].

29. *MTP* 29.132.

of my Father,' or, 'Depart, ye cursed, into everlasting fire.'"[30] According to Spurgeon, just as the Spirit presently convicts of sin and righteousness, in like manner, the Holy Spirit will convict at the final judgement. As Spurgeon described, the conviction of the Holy Spirit was painful, led to joy, and prefigured the Spirit's work in final judgement.

Living a Godly Life

Second, Spurgeon understood that the work of the Spirit in sanctification empowered the Christian to live a holy life. Spurgeon variously referred to this aspect of sanctification as Christian living, practical holiness, or godliness. In his sermon on Romans 8:14, Spurgeon explained that the "Holy Ghost leads those who are children of God into *vital godliness*—the mystic essence of spiritual life."[31] This meant for Spurgeon that the Spirit's sanctification enabled Christians to participate in spiritual practices such as prayer, Bible reading, or actions useful for the kingdom of God. Spurgeon asserted, "There is something for everyone of us to do, a talent committed to the charge of every believer," and "if we have the Spirit of God dwelling in us he will tell us what the Lord has appointed us to perform, he will strengthen us for the doing of it, and set his seal and blessing upon it when it is done."[32] Thus, any godly act of the Christian is a result of the sanctification of the Holy Spirit. As Spurgeon described in his May 13, 1860 sermon, "There was never yet a heavenly thought, never yet a hallowed deed, never yet a consecrated act acceptable to God by Jesus Christ, which was not worked in us by the Holy Ghost. Thou hast worked all our works in us."[33] The Holy Spirit, in sanctification, empowers and causes the Christian to live a godly life.

---

30. *MTP* 29.132.
31. *MTP* 21.126.
32. *MTP* 21.127.
33. *NPSP* 6.230.

Holiness Perfected

Third, Spurgeon understood that sanctification was completed in the Christian at the moment of physical death. Spurgeon was distraught at the presence of sin in his own life, and he longed for the moment when he would be fully sanctified by the Holy Spirit. Two days before his twenty-first birthday, Spurgeon considered how, at the moment of his physical death, the Holy Spirit would complete the work of sanctification: "Oh! happy hour! may it be hastened! Just before I die, sanctification will be finished; but not till that moment shall I ever claim perfection in myself."[34] Spurgeon longed to be "washed white, clean, pure, perfect," to be "free from all dross, and fine like a wedge of pure gold," and to have "that last purification, and come up from Jordan's stream most white from the washing."[35] He believed that when that day came, he would be able to claim "in a double sense, 'Great God, I am clean—through Jesus's blood I am clean, through the Spirit's work I am clean too!'"[36] He lamented over the reality of sin in the Christian, but he was confident that, at the moment of physical death, the Holy Spirit would perfect the work of holiness in the Christian, thus enabling the Christian to stand forever before the holy God. Therefore, Spurgeon announced, "Must we not extol the power of the Holy Ghost in thus making us fit to stand before our Father in heaven?"[37] Spurgeon not only desired sinlessness in his own life, but he constantly warned other Christians of sin that grieves the Holy Spirit.

Conclusion

Spurgeon believed that sanctification was a particular work of the Holy Spirit—the divine Sanctifier—who is the person of God that, after giving new life in regeneration, convicts the Christian of sin, causes him or her to live a holy life, and perfects the Christian in holiness at the moment of physical death. Ever weary of sin in

---

34.   *NPSP* 1.235.

35.   *NPSP* 1.235.

36.   *NPSP* 1.235.

37.   *NPSP* 1.235.

the Christian, and hopeful that the Spirit would finish his work of sanctification, Spurgeon commended:

> The faith which is wrought in us by the Holy Ghost is the greatest sin-killer under heaven. By the grace of God it affects the inmost heart, changes the desires and the affections, and makes the man a new creature in Christ Jesus.... Faith trusts God, and therefore loves him, and therefore obeys him, and therefore grows like him. It is the root of holiness, the spring of righteousness, the life of the just.[38]

In his final words of that November 11, 1883 sermon, Spurgeon prayed, "may God the Holy Ghost work in us more of that faith. Amen and Amen."[39]

---

38. *MTP* 29.616.

39. *MTP* 29.624.

11

"Temples of the Holy Spirit"
The Holy Spirit and Perseverance

It is written that we are the temples of the Holy Spirit: shall
the temples of the Holy Spirit become like the temples of Jove
or of Saturn? Shall they be given up to the moles and the bats,
degraded and defiled? God forbid! He that dwells there will drive
out the foe and maintain a shrine for Himself in purity. The Holy
Ghost has begun to sanctify us… and at the last the Spirit shall
not be defeated in a single heart wherein he came to dwell. Let
us rejoice, then, that when we consider the work of the Father,
Son, and Holy Spirit, it does seem impossible that the righteous
should be lost. They must, therefore, hold on their way.[1]

Spurgeon loved preaching on the topic of the final perseverance
of the Christian. In his estimation, the "one doctrine I have
preached more than another… is the doctrine of the perseverance
of the saints even to the end."[2] Doubtless, a main factor for
Spurgeon's insistence on this doctrine was the principal role it
played in his own conversion. In the conclusion of his March 7,
1872 sermon, Spurgeon affirmed that "one of the great leading
thoughts of my young life, the master thought that brought me
to the Saviour, was belief in the doctrine of final perseverance."[3]

---

1.   *MTP* 13.262.

2.   *MTP* 18.337. For sermons on perseverance of the saints, see *NPSP* 2, sermon
75; *MTP* 10, sermon 554; *MTP* 13, sermon 749; *MTP* 15, sermon 872; *MTP* 18, sermon
1056; *MTP* 19, sermon 1111; *MTP* 23, sermon 1361; *MTP* 33, sermon 1945; *MTP* 33,
sermon 1959; *MTP* 35, sermon 2108; *MTP* 38, sermon 2253; and *MTP* 45, sermon 2607.

3.   *MTP* 18.347.

Even as he clung to the hope revealed in the doctrine of the final perseverance of the saints, Spurgeon also upheld and promoted it throughout his teaching ministry.

Two of Spurgeon's most insightful sermons on the doctrine of perseverance were his successive Thursday evening addresses on February 29 and March 7, 1872. In the first of these two sermons, Spurgeon argued that "it is only by continuing in the faith with which we began that we are proved to be partakers of the Lord Jesus Christ."[4] Incidentally, one of the phrases or explanations he made in the first sermon unintentionally caused a person who was new to the congregation to become unsure whether Spurgeon held to the doctrine of perseverance. Therefore, on learning of that response, Spurgeon clarified his position the following week with another sermon on the topic, and explained, "The one way by which a soul is saved is by that soul's abiding in Christ; if it did not abide in Christ, it would be cast forth as a branch and be withered. But, then, we know that they who are grafted into Christ will abide in Christ."[5] Spurgeon asserted that this abiding in Christ was solely "based on the operation of the Spirit of God."[6]

In an attempt at full clarity, on the third successive Thursday, on March 14, 1872, Spurgeon summarised the main points of the previous two Thursday sermons: "The one [sermon] admonished us to *perseverance* by holding fast; the other assured us of *preservation*, because we are fast held."[7]

Spurgeon refined and clarified his view on perseverance throughout the course of his ministry. Nevertheless, as these three sermons display, Spurgeon held to a twofold description of perseverance: 1) that the Christian must persevere in faith, and 2) that the Christian will be preserved. As we will find in this chapter, Spurgeon believed that both aspects of perseverance stood in complete dependence on the Holy Spirit. In the first, the Holy Spirit, as the divine comforter, empowers the Christian's

---

4. *MTP* 18.337.

5. *MTP* 18.337.

6. *MTP* 18.337.

7. *MTP* 18.409.

ability to persevere through life. In the second, the Christian's salvation is secured by the Holy Spirit's sealing.

The Anointing Oil of the Holy Spirit

After the Spirit, like the wind, regenerates the Christian and, like fire, purifies the Christian, then the "Holy Spirit comes, like the good Samaritan, and pours in the oil and the wine. And oh! what oil it is with which he anoints our head, and with which he heals our wounds!"[8] Through this anointing, as Spurgeon described, the Holy Spirit makes the Christian glad, causes the Christian to rejoice, and "binds up our sores, and wounds, and bruises, and makes us whole, and sets our feet upon a rock, and establishes our goings!"[9] Spurgeon's use of this image worked in two ways. First, he understood the Holy Spirit comforts Christians with "heavenly ointment" to enable them to endure to the end. The Spirit's anointing empowers the Christian to remain faithful to Christ throughout his or her life. Second, by this anointing, the Spirit declares that the Christian is established forever. As Spurgeon praised, the products of the Spirit's anointing are "joy in the Spirit, and peace, and love, and confidence, and assurance for ever."[10] In this way, the Holy Spirit both enables the Christian to persevere and ensures that the Christian will be preserved. This imagery of the Holy Spirit anointing the Christian with oil captured well Spurgeon's understanding of the Spirit's twofold work of perseverance.

The Spirit's Work in Perseverance

The remainder of this chapter will demonstrate how Spurgeon believed the Holy Spirit was involved in each facet of this twofold description of perseverance. First, Spurgeon maintained that the Holy Spirit is the comforter for the Christian as he or she perseveres in faith. Second, the Holy Spirit is the seal of the Christian, who guarantees the Christian's eternal perseverance.

---

8. *NPSP* 4.20.

9. *NPSP* 4.20.

10. *NPSP* 4.20.

Lastly, Spurgeon understood that the result of these two teachings was the Christian's assurance of salvation in Jesus Christ.

Perseverance in Faith

The Holy Spirit's role as comforter enables the Christian to persevere in the faith. Spurgeon's own life exhibited this aspect of perseverance that he taught. He faced the challenging realities of ministry, suffered various illnesses, and fought with depression on numerous occasions in his life.[11] Adding insult to injury, he was constantly embattled with ministerial controversies as he regularly fended off theological and personal attacks. When Spurgeon reflected on the trying times he faced, he acknowledged, "There are dungeons underneath the Castle of Despair as dreary as the abodes of the lost, and some of us have been in them."[12] He taught on perseverance from a theological perspective, but also as one who had to endure his own hardships. Spurgeon knew existentially that the only way one could endure through difficult times was to depend on the Holy Spirit as comforter.

The year 1888 was a particularly difficult one for Spurgeon. On January 18, the Baptist Union Council accepted Spurgeon's withdrawal from the union and voted to censure him.[13] In April of the same year, Spurgeon also withdrew from the London Baptist Association, and on May 23 his mother, Eliza Jarvis Spurgeon, died. The death of his mother hit Spurgeon the hardest. No doubt, his love for her was exemplified in the 1873 edition of *The Sword and the Trowel*, when he published an article titled "John Ploughman on Mothers."[14]

---

11. Many of his struggles can be seen in Charles H. Spurgeon, *The Suffering Letters of C H Spurgeon*, ed. Hannah Wyncoll (London: Wakeman Trust, 2016). For a description of several of the significant controversies of Spurgeon's life, see Murray, *The Forgotten Spurgeon*.

12. William Williams, *Personal Reminiscences of Charles Haddon Spurgeon* (London: The Religious Tract Society, 1895), 166.

13. While Spurgeon confessed in the February 1888 edition of *The Sword and the Trowel*, "I do not complain of the censure of the Council, or feel the least care about it," he also wrote a brief letter to his son Charles on February 25, 1888 in which he stated, "The Lord is with us, I am sure. May He be with you to-morrow in a very special way. Truth will pay her own charges though she costs dear for awhile" (*Letters* 85).

14. *S&T* 9.391–93.

Much of the content was a personal reflection on his mother's love and care for him. Spurgeon described, "Most men are what their mothers made them.… Every mother is a handsome woman to her own son. That man is not worth hanging who does not love his mother. When good women lead their little ones to the Savior, the Lord Jesus blesses not only the children, but their mothers as well."[15] Spurgeon submitted, "Good mothers are very dear to their children. There's no mother in the world like our own mother."[16]

It seems of little coincidence that Spurgeon's sermon, which was intended for reading on June 3, 1888, only twelve days after his mother's death, was titled "The Saddest of the Sad." In that sermon, he sympathised with those in the deepest of despairs, as one who had gone through the same: "Ah! there is no Bastille so awful as that which is built by despair, and kept under the custody of a crushed spirit. Many are the desponding ones whose eyes fail so that they cannot look up, or look out. To such I speak."[17] His consolation for those in that condition of life was simply, "May God speak through me by the Holy Spirit, the Comforter!"[18] Spurgeon attested from personal experience that the Holy Spirit, as the divine comforter, was the only one who could enable a Christian to persevere.

Further, Spurgeon depicted the Christian life as a journey filled with difficulties. He knew that the Christian life was treacherous, and that journeying safely through required inordinate stamina. As such, he argued, "It is not true that one act of faith is all, and that nothing is needed of daily faith, prayer, and watchfulness. Our doctrine is the very opposite, namely, that the righteous shall hold on his way; or, in other words, shall continue in faith, in repentance, in prayer, and under the influence of the grace of God."[19]

His point was not that these daily acts themselves were the cause of the Christian's perseverance, but that underneath

---

15. *S&T* 9.391–92.
16. *S&T* 9.392.
17. *MTP* 34.303.
18. *MTP* 34.303.
19. *MTP* 23.362.

them was God's grace for perseverance. Spurgeon summarised this point in his 1864 sermon on "Enduring until the End," when he explained, "But ye cannot persevere except by much watchfulness in the closet, much carefulness over every action, much dependence upon the strong hand of the Holy Spirit who alone can make you stand."[20] In the end, Spurgeon affirmed that the Holy Spirit alone is able to cause a Christian to persevere, even as the Christian journey requires utter dependence on the Spirit.

Spurgeon also believed that sometimes the Holy Spirit used difficulties to cause the Christian to depend more on the Spirit and less on oneself. In his March 8, 1863 sermon, Spurgeon referred to the Spirit as the "black angel of distress."[21] Even though the Spirit might at times use misery as a means of perseverance, Spurgeon explained, "In fact, if you look well at the black angel, as I have called him, you will see that he is not black, but exceedingly bright, for there is a gracious ministry in those loving sorrows, there is an angelic kindness in those loving cruelties (as some term them) by which God doth sometimes bring hardened sinners to himself."[22] The Spirit's aim was to bring the Christian through the distresses of life, perhaps even using them to create in the Christian more reliance on the Spirit. Indeed, Spurgeon explained, "Many a heart would break if the Spirit of God had not comforted it. Many of God's dear children would have utterly died by the way if he had not bestowed upon them his divine consolations to cheer their pilgrimage."[23] Ultimately, in order for the Christian to persevere in faith, the Holy Spirit worked as the divine comforter, which was a "very necessary work."[24]

Preservation by the Holy Spirit

Spurgeon also maintained with certainty that the Christian will be preserved in Jesus Christ by the Holy Spirit who operates as the Christian's seal. In this way, the Holy Spirit both ensures

20. *MTP* 10.96.
21. *MTP* 52.304.
22. *MTP* 52.304–05.
23. *MTP* 23.22.
24. *MTP* 23.22.

the eternal security of Christians and provides the Christian with assurance of his or her own salvation. The two key biblical passages that proved this for Spurgeon were Ephesians 1:13–14 and Hebrews 6:4–6.

According to Ephesians 1:13–14, Spurgeon believed that the Holy Spirit was himself the seal of the Christian, thus securing the Christian's eternal salvation. Spurgeon preached this text on March 19, 1876, and began by describing the complementary roles of Christ and the Holy Spirit in the work of the Christian's sealing. "The Spirit of God never takes the place of the Redeemer," Spurgeon argued, but "he exercises his own peculiar office, which is to take of the things of Christ and show them unto us, and not to put his own things in the place of Jesus."[25] The Holy Spirit applies to the Christian the blessings of redemption earned by Christ. At the same time, the Christian's perseverance was prefigured by the work of the Spirit in Christ. Before the Holy Spirit was the seal for the Christian, Spurgeon explained that the Spirit was first "the seal upon our Lord Jesus Christ… *for his perseverance even to the end.*"[26] Thus, just as Christ was sealed with the Holy Spirit, the Christian, who is "marked as the Lord's peculiar treasure," is likewise sealed.[27]

Based on Ephesians 1, Spurgeon believed that the Holy Spirit himself and all of his work toward the Christian is the Christian's seal. As Spurgeon argued, no single "operation of the Holy Spirit is to be regarded as the seal, but the whole of them together, as they prove his being within us, make up that seal."[28] Even more, Spurgeon concluded that it was the Spirit himself who is the seal of the Christian, and secures him or her in Christ. Spurgeon explained, "According to the text, as far as I can read it, here is a man who has believed in Jesus, and he desires a seal that God loves him: God gives him the Spirit, and that is all the seal he can wish for or expect. Nothing more is wanted, nothing else would

---

25. *MTP* 22.159.

26. *MTP* 22.163 (emphasis added).

27. *MTP* 22.160.

28. *MTP* 22.164.

be so good."[29] For Spurgeon, the Holy Spirit himself and all of his work sealed the Christian, thus securing the Christian's eternal salvation.

Further, Spurgeon defended his belief that the Holy Spirit, as the Christian's seal, would not allow a Christian to fall away from salvation. The primary text of Scripture on which Spurgeon based his teaching was Hebrews 6:4–6. Hebrews 6:6 speaks of those who "fall away." The identity of those who "fall away" has been a topic of much discussion throughout the history of Christianity. Two theologians who wrote on this topic and were particularly influential to Spurgeon were John Gill and John Owen. While Spurgeon acknowledged his indebtedness to the writings of both men, he diverged from their view on the identity of those described in Hebrews 6 who might "fall away." It is instructive about the care that Spurgeon took on every topic of biblical theology to see him disagree with these two men, for example, whom he eagerly endorsed as faithful Christian teachers. Contrary to Gill and Owen, Spurgeon understood this text to teach that a true Christian could fall away—that is, for "the Holy Spirit entirely to go out of a man."[30] If this occurred, it would be impossible for that person to be renewed to Christian faith. While Spurgeon held to this possibility, he also maintained, "There never has been a case of it yet, and therefore I cannot describe it from observation."[31] While the interpretation of Gill and Owen held that no true Christian could fall away, Spurgeon argued that no true Christian had fallen away.

Regardless of his interpretation of this specific biblical passage, the true promise of perseverance was the presence of the Holy Spirit: "If, my hearer, the Holy Ghost dwells in your soul, and that Holy Ghost does not sanctify you and keep you to the end, what else can be tried? Ask the blasphemer whether he knows a being, or dares to suppose a being superior to the Holy Spirit! Is there a being greater than Omnipotence?"[32] With the Holy Spirit the

---

29. *MTP* 22.163.

30. *NPSP* 2.172.

31. *NPSP* 2.172.

32. *NPSP* 2.174.

Christian is sure to persevere, but without him one is sure to fail. As Spurgeon explained, the Holy Spirit "is not to you a luxury, but a necessity: you must have him, or you die; you must have him, or you are damned, ay, and with a double damnation."[33] Spurgeon was confident that the Holy Spirit, as the seal of the Christian, would never allow the Christian to fall away from Christ.

Assurance of Faith

Finally, Spurgeon believed that assurance of faith constituted a blessed and great gift of God to the Christian. Whereas perseverance indicated both the call for the Christian to persevere in faith and the promise of God to preserve the Christian, assurance was the Christian's confidence that he or she would endure and was eternally secure in Christ. Spurgeon himself was not immune to doubting his own salvation, but his greater concern was that many Christians in his context struggled with confidence in their salvation. Therefore, he reminded his listeners that assurance was found in the indwelling presence of the Holy Spirit.

Spurgeon maintained that the greatest indication for assurance of salvation was the indwelling presence of the Holy Spirit. Therefore, when he addressed this topic, he called all to consider whether they had sensed the presence of the Spirit. In his 1888 sermon, "The Blessing of Full Assurance," Spurgeon described, "If the Spirit of God be in you, he is the earnest of your eternal inheritance."[34] In an age of skepticism, where science and reason were being looked to for security, Spurgeon led Christians to put their trust in God. The Holy Spirit himself provided the Christian's confidence in God's promise of salvation. The indwelling presence of the Holy Spirit was the mark of a true Christian, and the foundation of assurance.

Even more, Spurgeon believed that the Holy Spirit would provide to the Christian the knowledge of his indwelling presence. In this way, the Christian's assurance is thoroughly a work of the Holy Spirit—the Holy Spirit's indwelling presence is

33.   *MTP* 13.131.
34.   *MTP* 34.269.

itself the assurance of salvation for the Christian, and the Holy Spirit makes known his indwelling presence to the Christian, which produces the Christian's assured confidence of his or her salvation. According to Spurgeon, it is primarily through the biblical doctrine of election that the Spirit accomplishes this latter part of the work of assurance, namely, making known to the Christian the indwelling presence of the Spirit. Spurgeon believed there was certainty of salvation among Christians who understood themselves as chosen by God. However, as Spurgeon explained, "Until the Spirit opens the eye to read, until the Spirit imparts the mystic secret, no heart can know its election. No angel ever revealed to any man that he was chosen of God; but the Spirit doth it."[35] In order to provide the Christian with this assurance, the Holy Spirit causes one to understand and believe that he or she has been eternally elected by God in Jesus Christ. The result of this knowledge, then, is confidence in God's sovereign will. Therefore, for Spurgeon, the complete work of assurance was dependent on the Holy Spirit as it is based on the indwelling presence of the Holy Spirit, and then revealed to the Christian by the Spirit's illumination and teaching.

Conclusion

In his October 9, 1859 sermon entitled "Grieving the Holy Spirit," Spurgeon preached on perseverance as the Spirit's application of the work. The Holy Spirit seals the Christian and by this sealing the Christian is preserved through life and emboldened to believe, "We shall hold on our way."[36] Even though sin in the Christian grieves the Holy Spirit, still the Spirit sustains the Christian with his divine comfort and indwelling presence. Thus, Spurgeon praised, "When I think how often you and I have let the devil in, I wonder the Spirit has not withdrawn from us. The final perseverance of the saints is one of the greatest miracles on record; in fact, it is the sum total of miracles."[37]

---

35. *NPSP* 5.212.

36. *NPSP* 5.429.

37. *NPSP* 5.428.

12

"The Vicar of Christ"
The Holy Spirit and the Church

We have fancied that the bodily presence of Christ would make us blessed, and confer innumerable boons; but according to our text, the presence of the Holy Ghost working in the Church, is more expedient for the Church.... my brethren, the Holy Spirit, the vicar of Christ, dwells everywhere;... and through that Holy Spirit Christ keeps His promise, "Where two or three are met together in my name, there am I in the midst of them."[1]

Spurgeon grew up in the church. From his childhood years, he saw firsthand his grandfather serving as the minister of the Congregationalist church in Stambourne, and he spent many of his childhood days in and around the meeting house. When he was a boy, Spurgeon drew a sketch of that old meeting house, and forty-five years later, when he closed his eyes, he could still picture every detail of it, even the peg at the back of the pulpit that held the preacher's hat. The boy Spurgeon knew what the church building was like when it was empty, which suggests that he also recognised from an early age that church ministry was more than preaching, as most any child of a minister can attest. As he came into his ministry years, his love for the church grew, his theology of the church developed, and he came to understand even more that his role as a pastor meant serving in the Lord's church in the variety of ways that a pastor is called to do.

---

1. *MTP* 10.331–32.

A significant component of Spurgeon's ecclesiology was his understanding that the Holy Spirit was present in the church in a unique and intentional way. Preaching on John 16:7, Spurgeon instructed, "We have fancied that the bodily presence of Christ would make us blessed, and confer innumerable boons; but according to our text, the presence of the Holy Ghost working in the Church, is more expedient for the Church."[2] While Christ in bodily form can only dwell in one place, the Holy Spirit "dwells everywhere," and especially dwells in the church. Spurgeon described that the Holy Spirit, who is the Spirit of Christ, was "the vicar of Christ," such that by his presence the church is enabled to "sweetly enjoy" the continued presence of Christ among them.[3] This understanding of the presence of the Holy Spirit was how Spurgeon understood the promise of Christ to his church to be fulfilled: "Where two or three are met together in my name, there am I in the midst of them."[4] The Spirit's special presence in the church was the theological foundation from which Spurgeon built his understanding of the Spirit's work within the church.

The previous four chapters addressed Spurgeon's understanding of the work of the Spirit toward the individual Christian. The present chapter, along with the chapters to follow, will explore Spurgeon's teaching on the work of the Spirit in the context of the church. Spurgeon believed that the Holy Spirit's work through the church primarily involved the ordinances, preaching, evangelism, and spiritual gifts. While Spurgeon never directly suggested that the Spirit's work in the church was pictured in the Spirit's work toward the individual Christian, the way he described the work of the Spirit in the church mirrored his understanding of the work of the Spirit in the Christian. For instance, as Spurgeon explained, whereas in regeneration the Spirit comes to dwell in the life of the Christian, so too the Spirit's presence is the life of the church; just as the Spirit opens the eyes of the Christian through conversion, so too the Spirit enlightens the church through the ordinances;

---

2. *MTP* 10.331.
3. *MTP* 10.332.
4. *MTP* 10.332.

just as the Spirit sanctifies the Christian, he also makes the church holy through preaching and evangelism; and as the Spirit promises to secure the Christian for final salvation, so too the Spirit bestows gifts to his people for the building up of the church. As the foundation for the chapters that follow, the present chapter will show that Spurgeon believed that the Holy Spirit formed the church, unites the church, and sustains the church. Finally, we will see that Spurgeon believed the Spirit works in the church especially by raising up and empowering the church's ministers.

The Spirit in the Church

According to Spurgeon, the Spirit's direct work in the church was to create, unite, and sustain the church. Just like the Spirit's initial work in the Christian was regeneration, similarly the Spirit's initial act toward the church was its creation. In his sermon on John 14:17, Spurgeon referenced Acts 2 and commented, "My brethren, *we have seen the operations of the Holy Spirit in the church at large.* It was the Holy Spirit who at the very first formed the church; it is he who called out the chosen ones, quickened them, made them living stones fit to be built together for a habitation of God through the Spirit."[5] As with regeneration, the Spirit gives life to the church, because "he is the very breath of the church."[6] To Spurgeon, the first work of the Spirit toward the church was its formation.

Spurgeon also believed that the Holy Spirit was the bond of unity among the church. In his February 6, 1870 sermon, Spurgeon explained that *esprit de corps* refers to the reality in which "men are moved to desire the prosperity of the community to which they belong."[7] While people have a natural tendency to identify among communities, in a similar and greater way, "The Holy Spirit makes us feel one with Christ's church."[8] To Spurgeon, the presence of the Holy Spirit trumped denominational affiliations, secondary theological positions, and local church preferences.

---

5. *MTP* 13.314 (emphasis added).

6. *MTP* 33.146.

7. *MTP* 16.81.

8. *MTP* 16.81.

In this way, the Spirit is *the* unifying element of the church. In his sermon "Unity in Christ," Spurgeon argued, "Christ's body is not made up of denominations, nor of presbyteries, nor of Christian societies; it is made up of saints chosen of God from before the foundation of the world, redeemed by blood, called by his Spirit, and made one with Jesus."[9] By creating and dwelling in the church, the Holy Spirit unites the church together as the body of Christ.

Lastly, Spurgeon believed that the Holy Spirit sustained the church. Spurgeon proved this point with the positive example of his ministry and the negative example of dying churches. In August of 1862, Spurgeon reflected on the ministry of the Metropolitan Tabernacle and credited the Holy Spirit for their success. He acknowledged, "When we, as a Church, first came out into broader light and more public notice, I bear my witness, we had an entire dependence upon the Holy Ghost."[10] Without the Holy Spirit, no work of the church was effectual. Therefore, Spurgeon exhorted:

> Nothing can ye do ye ministers of God, nothing ye faithful watchmen of Jerusalem, nothing can ye do ye teachers of youth, nothing ye heralds of the cross in foreign fields, nothing ye ten thousands who are willing to give all your substance, your time, and your talents, absolutely nothing can ye accomplish until God the Holy Spirit comes.[11]

Spurgeon called his church to depend continually on the Holy Spirit, as they had done from the start of his pastoral tenure, because the Holy Spirit alone can sustain the life of the church.

Conversely, Spurgeon's lament over dying churches, those from which the Holy Spirit had departed, also proved his belief that the Holy Spirit sustains the church. Spurgeon conveyed that a church's denial of the truth and authority of Scripture grieved the Holy Spirit such that the Spirit would depart from the midst of that church. And when the Spirit departed such congregations,

---

9.   *MTP* 12.4.

10.   *MTP* 8.465.

11.   *MTP* 8.465.

they began to die. On October 9, 1859, less than two months after the foundation stone was laid for the Metropolitan Tabernacle, Spurgeon described the recent historical context of England: "Throughout England, at least some four or five years ago, an almost universal torpor had fallen upon the visible body of Christ."[12] As Spurgeon saw it, the sins of the church had driven away the presence of the Holy Spirit—"He is grieved, and he is gone."[13] Fearing that history may be repeating itself some twenty-seven years later, Spurgeon prayed, "Come, Holy Spirit, heavenly Dove, brood over the dark, disordered church as once thou didst over chaos, and order shall come out of confusion, and the darkness shall fly before the light."[14]

Spurgeon maintained that dying churches were congregations that grieved the Holy Spirit, and, consequently, from which the Holy Spirit departed. Conversely, the only hope for a church's continued fruitful existence was the presence of the Holy Spirit. Indeed, the longer Spurgeon pastored the more earnestly he prayed, "Oh! if I might but live to see the Church of God recognize the power of the Holy Ghost; if I could but see her cast aside the grave clothes which she has so long persisted in wearing... if I could see her depend upon the Holy Ghost."[15] It was the Spirit's presence in the church that Spurgeon most desired for the church: "Only let the Spirit be with us, and we have all that is wanted for victory. Give us his presence, and everything else will come in its due season for the profitable service of the entire church."[16] Spurgeon believed that the Holy Spirit created and sustained the life of the church, and without the Spirit the church was sure to die.

The Spirit and the Minister

Spurgeon knew how essential the role of the minister was to the church, and as such he believed that the Holy Spirit especially

12. *NPSP* 5.431.
13. *NPSP* 5.431.
14. *MTP* 32.488.
15. *MTP* 13.132.
16. *MTP* 31.488.

works to raise up ministers for the church and to empower each minister in the task. In the first place, Spurgeon was so committed to the idea that the Holy Spirit himself created ministers for the church, and so leery about the idea that the church on its own would be credited with this act, that he rejected the idea of ordination. His observations of the ordination process in the Church of England led him to dismiss the practice altogether, and argue, "A true minister is a creation of the God of heaven."[17] In fairness, Spurgeon admitted, "Independency is as weak as Episcopacy on this point."[18] He also understood that the church had a part to play in the calling of ministers. However, while the church had a role in appointing its ministers, it must be careful not to attempt what only the Holy Spirit can do. Spurgeon insisted:

> God alone ordains ministers; all that the Church can do is to recognize them. We cannot make them at our colleges; we cannot make them by the laying on of hands, nor even by the choice of the Church. God must make them; God must ordain them; it is only for the Church to perceive God's work and cheerfully to submit to his choice.[19]

Furthermore, Spurgeon believed that the minister must be constantly empowered by the Holy Spirit in order to be effective in his ministry. When Spurgeon first came to pastor in the city, he was mocked and ridiculed. Nevertheless, when he came to the city the Holy Spirit empowered his ministry. Spurgeon admitted to his congregation, "Joyously would I receive again the jeer, the sneer, the constant slander that was heaped upon my devoted head, if I might have back again your entire dependence upon the Holy Ghost."[20] He recognised that this dependence would mean the church "should have to be baptized in blood... put no confidence in State or power—rely no longer upon eloquence and learning... and her followers should again be the 'base things of

---

17. *MTP* 8.459.

18. *MTP* 8.459.

19. *MTP* 8.459.

20. *MTP* 8.466.

this world, and the things that are not.'"[21] He knew this kind of reliance on the Spirit would likely mean a loss of worldly status, or even appearing foolish in the world's estimation. Spurgeon willingly accepted the cost of giving up status in the world's eyes, even if "her ministers should again be fishermen," so that in exchange "the free Spirit of the living God ruled everywhere."[22] Spurgeon believed that if being a minister of the gospel meant being completely dependent on the Holy Spirit and losing worldly status, then that was a worthwhile price to pay for the minister and the church.

Instead of worldly acclamation, the church needed "fire to quicken her ministers, to give zeal and energy to all her members."[23] This fire that Spurgeon desired was the Holy Spirit himself. Therefore, to his fellow ministers Spurgeon instructed, "*We must give ourselves to prayer before our work, in our work, and after our work*," and to the church he instructed, "bear [the preacher] up in your supplications, feeling that your attendances at the house of God will be all vanity, and the coming together of the people will be as nothing, unless God the Holy Ghost is pleased to bless the Word."[24] This "habit of prayer," as Spurgeon described, must be constant among the ministers and the church, "so that you neither begin any service for God, nor carry it on, nor conclude it, without crying to the Lord for his Holy Spirit to make the work effectual by his almighty power."[25] Seven days before his thirtieth birthday, he declared, "If there were only one prayer which I might pray before I died, it should be this; 'Lord, send thy Church men filled with the Holy Ghost, and with fire.'"[26] Spurgeon desired that the church would have ministers empowered by the Holy Spirit, and he believed that the Spirit effectually worked in and through the church by creating and empowering such ministers.

---

21. *MTP* 13.132.
22. *MTP* 13.132.
23. *MTP* 10.336.
24. *MTP* 38.112 (emphasis added).
25. *MTP* 38.113.
26. *MTP* 10.337.

Conclusion

Spurgeon understood that the Holy Spirit gave birth to, unites, and sustains the church, and then works in the church especially by creating and empowering its ministers. According to Spurgeon, everything good that occurred in the church depended on the Holy Spirit. Thus, he urged his congregation, "Let us adore the third Person of the Trinity in Unity, and think of him often with deep reverence in our spirits, so that we never go to work, nor to prayer, nor even to the singing of a hymn, without seeking that he would himself be the life of the holy engagement."[27] As Spurgeon once described, "Brethren, the more than golden treasure of the church is the Holy Spirit."[28]

27. *MTP* 35.53.

28. *MTP* 13.315.

13

"The Spirit of God Witnessing"
The Holy Spirit and the Ordinances

> Other means, however, are made use of to bless men's souls.
> For instance, the two ordinances of Baptism and the Lord's
> Supper. They are both made a rich means of grace.... There
> must be something, then, beyond the outward ceremony; there
> must, in fact, be the Spirit of God, witnessing through the water,
> witnessing through the wine, witnessing through the bread,
> or otherwise none of these things could be means of grace to
> our souls.[1]

Spurgeon's theology of baptism and the Lord's Supper was
based on biblical convictions, but was also sharpened by key
events in his early life: namely, his childhood experience in a
Congregational church, a conversation he had as a teenager with
an Anglican priest, and even through theological disagreement
with his parents. First, Spurgeon was baptised as an infant in
his grandfather's church, and, while he had confidence in the
appropriateness of his grandfather's ministerial acumen, from an
early age he viewed infant baptism with some level of strangeness,
even thinking the baptismal basin was "originally intended for a
punch-bowl."[2] Later, as a fourteen-year-old student at a Church
of England school, his teacher, in an effort to send the boy on
a research journey for personal discovery, challenged Spurgeon
to show why the baptismal theology of the Church of England

---

1. *NPSP* 5.211–212.
2. *Autobiography* 1.15.

117

was correct. After his research, the boy Spurgeon returned to the teacher in defeat: "I could not find it,—I was beaten."[3] In the wake of this experience, Spurgeon the teenager "resolved, from that moment, that if ever Divine grace should work a change in me, I would be baptized."[4]

Following his conversion experience, Spurgeon was resolved to keep his adolescent commitment and receive believer's baptism by immersion. Not surprisingly, his Congregationalist parents, though certainly grateful for his conversion, were reluctant to support his desire to be baptised. His father was especially uneasy to grant approval.[5] As Spurgeon waited for Spring to usher in warmer weather for baptismal season to begin, he suspended himself from participating in the Lord's Supper. He believed that the Lord's Supper was reserved for those who were baptised, and now that he awaited his proper baptism he could not in good conscience come to the Lord's Table. On May 3, 1850, Spurgeon was baptised in the River Lark, and on May 5, the following Lord's Day, he "partook of the Lord's supper; a royal feast for me worthy of a King's son."[6]

Spurgeon believed that there were two ordinances of the church: baptism and the Lord's Supper. For him, these practices showed visibly the mysterious work of the Holy Spirit among the church. This chapter will argue that, according to Spurgeon, the Holy Spirit worked efficaciously through baptism and the Lord's Supper. First, we will see Spurgeon's understanding of the Spirit's role in baptism. Second, we will show how Spurgeon believed that the Holy Spirit provided communion between Jesus Christ and Christians through the Lord's Supper. The specific focus of this treatment of Spurgeon's theology is to demonstrate how he viewed the Holy Spirit in relation to these two ordinances. While there have been a number of helpful treatments of Spurgeon's

---

3. *Autobiography* 1.49.

4. *Autobiography* 1.50.

5. In a letter to his father on April 6, 1850, Spurgeon requested his father's approval for his desire to be baptised. On April 20, Spurgeon wrote another letter to his mother asking again for "either permission or refusal to be baptized" since he had received no response from his father to the previous letter (*Autobiography* 1.121–23).

6. *Autobiography* 1.135.

baptismal and Communion theologies, none have specifically addressed his view of the Spirit's role in them. [7]

Baptism and the Holy Spirit

Spurgeon believed that the Holy Spirit was at work in baptism as the baptised person entered into the symbol of the Spirit's regeneration. In fact, Spurgeon's understanding of the Holy Spirit's work in regeneration was the grounds for his rejection of baptismal regeneration, which ultimately guided his baptismal theology. In 1859, Spurgeon admitted, "It is very seldom that I even mention the subject of baptism in my preaching, for I find that many of my hearers learn the Scriptural teaching concerning it without much help from me."[8] Nevertheless, the most widely distributed sermon of Spurgeon's ministry was the one he preached on June 5, 1864, entitled "Baptismal Regeneration."[9] Despite the relative truth of his admission that he seldom taught on the topic of baptism, the "Baptismal Regeneration" sermon gave his baptismal theology widespread attention.

This section will argue that Spurgeon's primary concern in his baptismal theology was maintaining a proper understanding of the Holy Spirit's activity in salvation. The idea of baptismal regeneration was so concerning to Spurgeon because it diminished the Spirit's work in the Christian. In order to prove this point, we will look at Spurgeon's "Baptismal Regeneration" sermon and consider the basis of his argument.

First of all, Spurgeon was clear throughout his ministry that baptism did not accomplish that which it depicted, namely, the regeneration of a person by the Holy Spirit. Nevertheless, Spurgeon neither hesitated to recognise the importance of baptism, nor to

---

7. Three helpful resources are Nettles, *Living by Revealed Truth*, 268–73, 513–17; Morden, *Communion with Christ and His People*, 77–105; and Chang, *Spurgeon the Pastor*, 73–98. Morden stated that in Spurgeon's belief in the Lord's Supper, "Christ was present by the Holy Spirit;" however, he did not elaborate on that component of Spurgeon's theology (179). Outside of Morden's reference, the volumes did not address Spurgeon's understanding of the role of the Holy Spirit in baptism or the Lord's Supper.

8. *MTP* 47.349.

9. In his January 1875 article "Twenty Years of Published Sermons," Spurgeon explained, "Several sermons in the series have attained a remarkable circulation, but probably the principal one is that upon Baptismal Regeneration" (*S&T* 11.5).

call people who have believed on Jesus to be baptised. In this way, his theology of baptism was centred around the authority of Jesus Christ. According to Spurgeon, the reason that baptism was necessary, even though it did not accomplish in itself what it depicted, was because baptism was a command of Jesus Christ. In his 1884 sermon on 1 Kings 17, Spurgeon asked, "Will the baptism save me?"[10] He answered, "Assuredly not," but he urged his listeners to consider, "If Christ gives you the command—if you accept him as a King—you are bound to obey him."[11]

Spurgeon's 1864 "Baptismal Regeneration" sermon exemplified the fact that the primary concern of his baptismal theology was a proper understanding of the Holy Spirit's role in salvation. In this sermon, preached on Mark 16:15–16, Spurgeon rejected any notion of baptism working as a means of grace in and of itself.[12] He stated the premise of his sermon in the introduction, noting that "the great error which we have to contend with throughout England (and it is growing more and more), is one in direct opposition to my text, well known to you as the doctrine of baptismal regeneration. We will confront this dogma with the assertion, that BAPTISM WITHOUT FAITH SAVES NO ONE."[13]

The backbone of Spurgeon's argument was the use of the liturgical language for a baptismal service from the Book of Common Prayer. In his sermon, Spurgeon quoted the thanksgiving prayer which was to be said by the priest after the public baptism of infants: "*Then shall the priest say, 'We yield thee hearty thanks,*

---

10. *MTP* 31.179.

11. *MTP* 31.179.

12. Interestingly, the biblical passage used in the sermon text that sparked the baptismal regeneration controversy was Mark 16:9–20, which is now generally understood as a later addition to Mark's Gospel as it is absent in early manuscripts. For more on the ending of Mark, see Robert H. Stein, *Mark*, BECNT (Grand Rapids: Baker Academic, 2008), 727–28. On the one hand, understanding Mark 16:9–20 as a later addition challenges Spurgeon's argument given the authority he assumes on the text as Scripture. On the other hand, this fact makes his argument for believer's baptism less strenuous if he does not have to address the phrase, "He that believeth and is baptized shall be saved" (Mark 16:16), which he struggled to resolve. Overall, his argument against baptismal regeneration is neither destroyed nor proven if Mark 16:9–20 is a later addition since he did not base his argument solely on this passage.

13. *MTP* 10.315. In the original printed copy of the sermon, the final phrase of his statement was emphasised with all capital letters, as indicated in the quotation.

most merciful Father, that it hath pleased thee to regenerate this infant with thy Holy Spirit, to receive him for thine own child by adoption, and to incorporate him into thy holy Church.'"[14] For Spurgeon, the regeneration that was assured is a work that is only accomplished by the Holy Spirit and cannot in any way be helped along or initiated by baptism, or by any other means of human involvement. While the premise of the "Baptismal Regeneration" sermon was the need for faith in salvation, the underlying issue for Spurgeon in this controversy was that regeneration, which is completely a work of the Holy Spirit, was being attributed to the activity of baptism itself.

Spurgeon admitted that constructing a positive and robust theology of baptism was a challenge for him. In his 1889 sermon on Mark 16:16, Spurgeon conceded, "I did not make the text. Perhaps, if I had made it, I should have left out that piece about baptism; but I have had no hand in making the Bible."[15] Spurgeon was committed to following the commands of Scripture, and in Scripture he found the clear command of Christ to reserve baptism for believers only, even though the reasons for it remained unclear. So, on the one hand, Spurgeon believed that complicating the theology of the ordinances by reason or explanation could do more harm to the church than good. On the other hand, Spurgeon maintained a particular theology of baptism, and he felt his position was reliant on a simple reading of Scripture, which made it more accessible to the common person. While he did not empty baptism of all meaning, he also avoided an overly-realised theology in favor of believer's baptism.

Overall, Spurgeon's argument against baptismal regeneration set the tone and substance of his baptismal theology. He insisted that water could not regenerate a person because regeneration was solely a work of the Holy Spirit. In his May 8, 1859 sermon on "The Necessity of the Spirit's Work," just before he discussed the

---

14. *MTP* 10.316. Spurgeon was quoting from the 1552 edition of the Book of Common Prayer (emphasis added).

15. *MTP* 39.605. Spurgeon's admission that he would have preferred the Scriptures to have "left out that piece about baptism" is fascinating and ironic given that the manuscript evidence now indicates that Mark 16:9–20 was not in the original text.

ordinances, he described the need for the Holy Spirit to work in order for ministry to be effective. "Under the ministry," Spurgeon described, "dead souls are quickened, sinners are made to repent, the vilest of sinners are made holy, men who came determined not to believe are compelled to believe."[16] His point was, "It must be that the Spirit worketh in man through the ministry, or else such deeds would never be accomplished. You might as well expect to raise the dead by whispering in their ears, as hope to save souls by preaching to them, if it were not for the agency of the Spirit."[17] Then, keeping with the theme of the necessity of the Spirit's work in ministry, Spurgeon asserted, "Other means, however, are made use of to bless men's souls. For instance, the two ordinances of Baptism and the Lord's Supper."[18] He asked, "Can immersion in water have the slightest tendency to be blessed to the soul?"[19] Since the answer was "no," he argued, "There must be something, then, beyond the outward ceremony; there must, in fact, be the Spirit of God, witnessing through the water."[20] If any blessing came through baptism, Spurgeon reasoned that it must be attributed to the Holy Spirit.

Even more, belief in baptismal regeneration was a sin that grieved the Holy Spirit. In 1863, nine days after Spurgeon's twenty-ninth birthday, he preached a sermon on Genesis 9:16. In the opening lines of the sermon, Spurgeon argued, "The story of Noah's preservation in the ark, is a suggestive representation of salvation by our Lord Jesus Christ."[21] He described that the story of Noah's ark was "especially intended to depict that part of our salvation which lies in the washing of regeneration." Following his reading of 1 Peter 3:21, Spurgeon explained, "In the same way as baptism is the outward symbol of regeneration, so also is the ark." While he recognised that baptism "is a most significant picture of regeneration," he qualified that "it is in no sense the cause of the

16. *NPSP* 5.211.

17. *NPSP* 5.211.

18. *NPSP* 5.211.

19. *NPSP* 5.211.

20. *NPSP* 5.212.

21. *MTP* 9.361. Every quotation in the present paragraph is from this source.

new birth." This was, in Spurgeon's assessment, the "blunder of the Puseyites," that they considered "the outward manifestation of an accomplished fact, as though it were the means of creating that fact." Baptism, Spurgeon affirmed, "saves no one, except, as Peter says, *in figure*; but as a figure, it is eminently full of divine teaching." Spurgeon, then, depicted baptism as a symbol or figure, which pictured regeneration but could not accomplish it.

Spurgeon later returned to the language of symbolism in his 1878 sermon on Galatians 4:6, and explained, "The spirit and essence of the ordinance lie in the soul's entering into the symbol, in the man's knowing not alone the baptism into water, but the baptism into the Holy Ghost and into fire."[22] While baptism could not bring about regeneration, it was, for Spurgeon, a symbolic act whereby the Christian participates in a practice that images the work of the Holy Spirit. Spurgeon was adamant that the water of baptism could not affect regeneration, though the Holy Spirit worked prior to and through baptism to accomplish his purpose in the Christian. In his October 8, 1865 sermon, titled "A Blow for Puseyism," Spurgeon emphasised that under the quickening ministry of the Holy Spirit, the Christian is given new life, and the ordinances themselves are quickened. He stated, "A spiritual man cometh to baptism, and he is baptised, and he quickens the baptism; it becomes a real living baptism to him, for he has fellowship with Jesus Christ in it."[23] When a spiritual person enters into baptism, the Holy Spirit works through that event to profit the Christian. Though Spurgeon rejected any hint of baptismal regeneration, he maintained that the Spirit worked in the Christian through the symbol of the ordinance.

Nearly three years after preaching the "Baptismal Regeneration" sermon, Spurgeon reflected on the state of the doctrine. In his March 3, 1867 sermon, he asserted that "the error has worked itself to its full development, and reached such a climax, that every Christian man ought to give it his most earnest consideration."[24] Again, he urged, "We must give up baptizing

---

22.   *MTP* 24.532.

23.   *MTP* 11.561.

24.   *MTP* 13.129.

in order to regenerate, and administer it to those alone who profess to be already regenerate."[25] Since belief in and teaching of baptismal regeneration grieves the Holy Spirit, Spurgeon's recommended response to the doctrinal error was "to renounce authority, antiquity, taste, and opinion, and bow before the Holy Ghost alone!"[26] To Spurgeon, baptismal regeneration was a serious error because it grieved the Holy Spirit, and he would more readily accept uncertainty regarding the meaning and theology of baptism than to grieve the Holy Spirit by saying too much.

The Lord's Supper and the Holy Spirit

As with his theology of baptism, after his conversion, Spurgeon first began to work out his new theological convictions among his family. A concern over his theology of the Lord's Supper was especially present with his grandfather. In a letter Spurgeon wrote his mother on June 11, 1850, he explained, "Grandfather has written to me; he does not blame me for being a Baptist, but hopes I shall not be one of the tight-laced, strict-communion sort."[27] On this topic, Spurgeon was happy to relay, "In that, we are agreed. I certainly think we ought to forget such things in others when we have come to the Lord's table. I can, and hope, I shall be charitable to unbaptized Christians, though I think they are mistaken."[28] By this answer, Spurgeon was referring to those who were baptised as infants. While his conscience convicted him about his need to be baptised by immersion before receiving the Lord's Supper, he would not require that in others before joining with them at the Supper. His convictions regarding the proper way in which baptism and the Lord's Supper should be practiced did not change. Nevertheless, the Lord's Supper was a unifying element among Christians, including those who had been baptised as an infant or as a believer.

Spurgeon's theology of the Lord's Supper not only created tension among his family, but it also put him in contention with

25. *MTP* 13.128.
26. *MTP* 13.129.
27. *Letters* 24.
28. *Letters* 24.

the Church of England. As with his simple understanding of baptism, so too Spurgeon rejected any activity that complicated the practice of the Lord's Supper. As Nettles described, "Spurgeon did not believe that it was necessary for 'an ordained or recognized minister' to preside at the Lord's Supper. He considered this a bit of 'unmitigated popery.'"[29] In his 1874 *The Sword and the Trowel* article, "Fragments of Popery among Nonconformists," Spurgeon argued:

> Even now we know of churches which have dispensed with the Lord's Supper week after week because the pastor was ill, there being, of course, no other brother in the whole community who had grace enough to preside at the table, or administer the sacrament, as some of the brotherhood call it. When matters have gone so far, it is surely time to speak out against such worship of men.[30]

Given the nature of the Lord's Supper as communion with Christ, Spurgeon rejected unnecessary hindrances to a Christian's participation in the ordinance.

Moreover, Spurgeon flatly rejected the doctrine of the corporeal presence of Jesus Christ in the Supper. He referred to the view as "monstrously absurd," and if it were true it would be "a gross act of cannibalism and nothing better."[31] While he rejected belief in the corporeal presence, he argued that in the Lord's Supper Christians "in a real and spiritual sense, but not in a carnal sort… receive the Lord Jesus, as incarnate, and crucified, into their spirits, as they believe in him, love him, and are comforted by thoughts of him."[32] Again, in his sermon "The Witness of the Lord's Supper," Spurgeon taught of Christ's presence in the Supper: "We believe in the real presence, but not in the corporeal presence."[33] Spurgeon clarified:

---

29. Nettles, *Living by Revealed Truth*, 271.

30. *S&T* 10.267.

31. *MTP* 11.554–55.

32. *MTP* 11.555.

33. *MTP* 59.38.

By spiritual we do not mean unreal; in fact, the spiritual takes the lead in realness to spiritual men. I believe in the true and real presence of Jesus with His people: such presence has been real to my spirit. Lord Jesus, Thou Thyself hast visited me. As surely as the Lord Jesus came really as to His flesh to Bethlehem and Calvary, so surely does He come really by His Spirit to His people in the hours of their communion with Him.[34]

Spurgeon believed that at the Lord's Supper the spiritual presence of Christ is made real by and through the Holy Spirit.

The edifying result of the Supper was also a direct work of the Holy Spirit. For Spurgeon, the Holy Spirit himself was the "channel of all good which cometh into you."[35] As a result of the real presence of Christ in communion, the Holy Spirit "brings first peace, then rest, and then joy of soul."[36] Therefore, the blessings that come through the Lord's Supper are a work of the Spirit through communion. Spurgeon denied that there was anything in the bread or wine itself that could divinely bless the human being, but he affirmed, "yet doubtless the grace of God does go with both ordinances for the confirming of the faith of those who receive them, and even for the conversion of those who look upon the ceremony."[37] Given this reality, Spurgeon argued:

> There must be something, then, beyond the outward ceremony; there must, in fact, be the Spirit of God, witnessing through the water, witnessing through the wine, witnessing through the bread, or otherwise none of these things could be means of grace to our souls. They could not edify; they could not help us to commune with Christ; they could not tend to the conviction of sinners, or to the establishment of saints.[38]

Therefore, he reasoned, "There must, then, from these facts, be a higher, unseen, mysterious influence—the influence of the divine

---

34. Charles Spurgeon, *"Till He Come": Communion Meditations and Addresses* (London: Passmore & Alabaster, 1896), 17.

35. *MTP* 10.338.

36. *"Till He Come,"* 17–18.

37. *NPSP* 5.212.

38. *NPSP* 5.212.

Spirit of God."[39] Spurgeon believed that the Holy Spirit, by his presence and power, worked through the Lord's Supper to edify Christians and bring them into communion with Jesus Christ.

Conclusion

Spurgeon's theology of the Holy Spirit instructed his theologies of baptism and the Lord's Supper. In both ordinances, Spurgeon believed, the Holy Spirit works efficaciously to bring about any blessing depicted or conferred to the Christian. As baptism was a symbol for regeneration, regeneration itself was accomplished by the Holy Spirit alone. Likewise, the Holy Spirit works in the Lord's Supper to edify the Christian and to provide communion with Jesus Christ. Any spiritual blessing conferred to the Christian through this ordinance is a blessing accomplished directly by the Spirit who is the real presence of Christ in the Supper.

---

39. *NPSP* 5.212.

14

"The Live Coal from the Altar"
The Holy Spirit and Preaching

The Spirit of God is peculiarly precious to us, because he especially instructs us as to the person and work of our Lord Jesus Christ; and that is the main point of our preaching.… [W]e need the Spirit in another manner, namely, as the live coal from off the altar, touching our lips, so that when we have knowledge and wisdom to select the fitting portion of truth, we may enjoy freedom of utterance when we come to deliver it.… Oh, how gloriously a man speaks when his lips are blistered with the live coal from the altar.[1]

The watching world searched for an explanation for how Spurgeon, the "Essex Bumpkin," could carry such influence in preaching among a metropolitan congregation.[2] The first and most obvious explanation for the power of Spurgeon's preaching was the sound and ability of his voice. On March 23, 1855, Spurgeon wrote a letter to his friend, James Watts, and reflected on the throngs of people crowding the places where Spurgeon preached. He remarked, "I believe I could secure a crowded audience at dead of night in a deep snow."[3] In the letter, Spurgeon celebrated that his success in preaching was attributed to the Lord. Nevertheless, there was something about the sound of his voice that drew people to hear him. Spurgeon wrote, "I am always at it, and the people are teasing me almost to death to get me to

---

1. *Lectures* 3.5, 7.
2. Stead, "Mr. Spurgeon at Home," 11.
3. *Letters* 109.

let them hear my voice. It is strange that such a power should be in one small body to crowd Exeter Hall to suffocation, and block up the Strand, so that pedestrians have to turn down by-ways, and all other traffic is at a standstill."[4] When Spurgeon preached, he spoke with power, and the crowds flocked even if just to hear his voice.

Susannah, likewise, reflected on her husband's preaching as it developed in the early part of 1855.[5] She recalled, "Sometimes his voice would almost break and fail as he pleaded with sinners to come to Christ, or magnified the Lord in His sovereignty and righteousness."[6] Spurgeon must have struggled periodically with a failing voice because he kept a glass of chili vinegar on hand as a remedy if needed. On one particular occasion at Exeter, Susannah described that at the end of a sermon Charles "made a mighty effort to recover his voice; but utterance well-nigh tailed, and only in broken accents could the pathetic peroration be heard,—'Let my name perish, but let Christ's Name last for ever! Jesus! Jesus! JESUS! Crown Him Lord of all!'"[7] This was one of the last times that the preacher's voice would fail him.

"In after days," Susannah explained, "when the Lord had fully perfected for him that silver-toned voice which ravished men's ears, while it melted their hearts, there was seldom any recurrence of the painful scene I have attempted to describe."[8] For the remainder of his ministry, Spurgeon "spoke with the utmost ease, in the largest buildings, to assembled thousands, and, as a master musician playing on a priceless instrument, he could at will either charm his audience with notes of dulcet sweetness, or ring forth the clarion tones of warning and alarm."[9] Spurgeon playfully commented that "his throat had been macadamised," but there was no jesting about the power that accompanied his preaching. Certainly, the ability of his voice was a factor in his

---

4. *Letters* 108.
5. *Autobiography* 2.20.
6. *Autobiography* 2.20.
7. *Autobiography* 2.20.
8. *Autobiography* 2.20.
9. *Autobiography* 2.20.

preaching success; however, Spurgeon believed the true power and effectiveness of preaching came from the Holy Spirit as he preached Christ from the Scriptures.

Spurgeon defined Christian preaching as proclaiming Christ from Scripture, and he believed that the Holy Spirit worked efficaciously through this preaching to convert sinners and sustain Christians. He understood that preaching was the primary means through which the gospel was proclaimed in the world, and by which the people of God were formed in godliness. He believed that the Holy Spirit was the agent responsible for accomplishing these ends.

After an introduction to the topic, this chapter will provide Spurgeon's definition of preaching. Next, this chapter will argue that Spurgeon believed preaching was, as the sword of the Spirit, the primary means by which the Spirit accomplished his work in and through the church. Lastly, this chapter will demonstrate Spurgeon's belief that the Spirit accomplished his aim in preaching by providing the sermon content to the preacher, empowering the act of preaching, and applying the sermon to the minds and hearts of the listeners.

Preaching Scripture, Showing Christ

Spurgeon was committed to Scripture as the primary authority in the Christian life, and he determined that his preaching ministry would only teach from the Bible. In his 1891 address at the Pastor's College conference, the last of these addresses he gave prior to his death, Spurgeon took 1 Timothy 6:12 as the theme verse, and exhorted his fellow pastors to follow Paul's example in fighting the good fight. In the opening portion of the address, Spurgeon defended Scripture as the Word of God, sufficient and authoritative for the Christian, and inexhaustible for the preacher. Speaking from experience, he celebrated that the simple preaching of God's Word brought about the conversion of many persons in his own ministry. He exhorted the pastors there to resolve to know the Bible better, to quote and reference

Scripture even more in sermons, and to "preach nothing but the Word of God."[10]

As he read and interpreted the Bible, Spurgeon believed that Jesus Christ was the central theme of all Scripture. Since Scripture formed the basis of Spurgeon's preaching ministry, and since Jesus was the central theme of his biblical hermeneutic, therefore Jesus Christ was the consistent theme of his sermons. Preaching on Sunday, November 12, 1865, at Cornwall Chapel, Spurgeon explained: "Faith cometh by hearing, and hearing by the Word of God. Christ himself is the essential Word, and the preaching of Christ Jesus is the operative Word.... Hence the necessity of continually preaching the Word of God."[11] As Spurgeon later explained in his sermon on John 15:5, "A sermon without Christ as its beginning, middle, and end is a mistake in conception and a crime in execution."[12] Likewise, the word of warning in his exposition on Acts 13:22–25 demonstrated his point of preaching Christ. Reflecting on Paul's sermon in the synagogue at Pisidia, Spurgeon explained:

> [Paul] had come by way of Old Testament history to Christ, and by way of John the Baptist to Christ; and that is how the preacher of the gospel should travel. On whatever road he journeys, his terminus must be Christ. The motto of all true servants of God must be, "We preach Christ, and him crucified." A sermon without Christ in it is like a loaf of bread without any flour in it. No Christ in your sermon, sir? Then go home, and never preach again until you have something worth preaching.[13]

The Sword of the Spirit

Preaching was, for Spurgeon, the primary means of the Holy Spirit's work through the church. While Spurgeon referred to both Scripture and preaching as "the sword of Spirit," his double use of the phrase emphasised his belief in the Spirit's work to

---

10. *GFW* 25.
11. *MTP* 11.640.
12. *MTP* 27.598.
13. *MTP* 50.430–31.

bring salvation through "first and foremost…the preaching of the Word of God!"[14] As Spurgeon stated in his May 8, 1859 sermon, "More men are brought to Christ by preaching than by anything else; for it is God's chief and first instrument. This is the sword of the Spirit, quick and powerful, to the dividing asunder of the joints and marrow."[15]

Spurgeon picked up the theme again in his April 19, 1891 sermon on "the Sword of the Spirit." In this sermon, Spurgeon mainly considered how the Scriptures functioned as the Spirit's sword. He described:

> The Word of God which is to be our weapon is of noble origin; for IT IS THE "SWORD OF THE SPIRIT.".… The Holy Ghost has made this Book himself: every portion of it bears his initial and impress; and thus he has a sword worthy of his own hand, a true Jerusalem blade of heavenly fabric. He delights to use a weapon so divinely made, and he does use it right gloriously.[16]

When a preacher utilises the Scriptures in his sermons he bears this sword and uses it. As Spurgeon once described, the Holy Spirit gives the preacher the "sword of the Spirit," and will "teach you how to use it."[17] The metaphor of the "Sword of the Spirit" was a vivid reminder for Spurgeon that the Holy Spirit gives the preacher the Scripture, which is his sword, and then teaches the preacher how to use the sword effectively in preaching.

But how, exactly, does the Holy Spirit accomplish his work? According to Spurgeon, the Holy Spirit was active in three primary ways: 1) the preparation of the sermon, 2) the execution of preaching, and 3) the application of the preached sermon in the lives of God's people. In these ways, the Holy Spirit empowered the preacher to illuminate Scripture, and enabled the hearer to comprehend its message. This understanding of the Spirit's role in preaching shows how Spurgeon believed the Holy Spirit was at work through the church's most significant activity.

---

14. *NPSP* 5.210.

15. *NPSP* 5.210.

16. *MTP* 37.230, 233.

17. *MTP* 32.491.

Sermon Preparation

Spurgeon depended on the Holy Spirit to provide him with content to preach. The task of planning the Sunday gathering was, for Spurgeon, of immense importance. In his *Lectures to My Students*, Spurgeon instructed, "I trust, my brethren, that we all feel very deeply the importance of conducting every part of divine worship with the utmost possible efficiency."[18] While all the elements of the service were critically significant to Spurgeon, he believed that the selection of the sermon text was a most serious task. His regular sermon preparation routine was to plan the Sunday morning sermon the night before, and the Sunday evening sermon after the Sunday morning service. The timing of this preparation might seem late in relation to the preaching event, but it was not an act of procrastination on Spurgeon's part. Rather, in Spurgeon's opinion planning out sermon texts or topics too far in advance was dismissive of the Spirit's role in providing the preacher with the sermon content at the proper time.

On November 5, 1857, Spurgeon preached a sermon on "The Work of the Holy Spirit." In that sermon he explained that his plan had been "on succeeding evenings, at different times, as God the Holy Spirit shall guide me, to enter more fully into the subject of the work of the Spirit from the beginning even to the end."[19] However, he changed his mind, and admitted that it was "no use your expecting me to preach a course of sermons. I know a great deal better than that. I don't believe God the Holy Spirit ever intended men to publish three months before hand, lists of sermons that they were going to preach."[20] The preacher should look for his sermons "as the Israelites looked for the manna, day by day."[21]

In his lecture "On the Choice of a Text," Spurgeon slightly amended his position on planning sermons in advance, which he had advocated in his November 5, 1857 sermon. When asked whether it was a good thing to "publish *lists of projected sermons*,"

---

18. *Lectures* 1.84.

19. *NPSP* 4.106.

20. *NPSP* 4.106.

21. *NPSP* 4.106.

Spurgeon acknowledged, "Every man in his own order. I am not a judge for others; but I dare not attempt such a thing, and should signally fail if I were to venture upon it."[22] Nevertheless, he also recognised, "Many eminent divines have delivered valuable courses of sermons upon pre-arranged topics," but, "[W]e are not eminent, and must counsel others like ourselves to be cautious how they act."[23]

In the November 5, 1857 sermon, Spurgeon indicated it was a poor practice to select a series of sermons in advance, but in his lecture he held that, though one should generally avoid the practice, ministers have the liberty to select texts in advance. Overall, Spurgeon expressed to his students, "I am jealous of anything which should hinder your daily dependence upon the Holy Spirit."[24] In regard to the preacher and his sermon topics, Spurgeon believed that "the choice of the text should rest with the all-wise Spirit of God."[25]

Spurgeon was convinced that the Holy Spirit could even impress upon the preacher's mind content for the sermon in miraculous ways or at the moment just before he begins preaching. There were many times in Spurgeon's ministry when he struggled on Saturday evening to plan the content of the following morning's sermon. On one particular Saturday night, Spurgeon had decided to preach on Psalm 110:3. After he had stayed up very late consulting "all the Commentaries he then possessed, seeking light from the Holy Spirit upon their words and his own thoughts," he was "utterly worn out and dispirited, for all his efforts to get at the heart of the text were unavailing."[26] His wife Susannah convinced him to sleep and finish in the morning, but while he was asleep Susannah heard her husband talking, and recognised him to be preaching in his sleep. She took the opportunity to write down what she heard. When he awoke, Susannah told him what had happened and gave him her notes from the preacher's nocturnal exposition.

---

22. *Lectures* 1.99.

23. *Lectures* 1.99.

24. *Lectures* 1.100–01.

25. *Lectures* 1.89.

26. *Autobiography* 2.188.

Spurgeon exclaimed, "Why! that's just what I wanted... that is the true explanation of the whole verse! And you say I preached it in my sleep? It is wonderful."[27] While this event was not normative in Spurgeon's sermon preparation, he believed the Holy Spirit could provide content for a sermon through supernatural means.

Further, Spurgeon taught that the Holy Spirit could provide the preacher the topic for the sermon up to the moment that he began preaching. In a lecture, Spurgeon expressed, "Under certain circumstances you will be absolutely compelled to cast away the well-studied discourse, and rely upon the present help of the Holy Spirit, using purely extempore speech."[28] After relaying the story of Kingman Nott who experienced that very thing among a group of "young men and boys of the roughest type," Spurgeon urged, "Brethren, I beseech you, believe in the Holy Ghost, and practically carry out your faith."[29] He told his students, "Every Holy Ghost preacher, I have no doubt, will have such recollections clustering around his ministry."[30] Of course, this dependence on the Holy Spirit did not mean a preacher should neglect the proper study of the Bible. In his lecture on the use of commentaries, Spurgeon exhorted, "It seems odd, that certain men who talk so much of what the Holy Spirit reveals to themselves, should think so little of what he has revealed to others."[31] Certainly, Spurgeon modelled in his own life a great appreciation for the writings of faithful Christians, both contemporary and historical, who were filled by the Spirit in their explanations of Scripture. Nevertheless, Spurgeon believed that the Holy Spirit's role in preaching includes his provision of the content of the sermon, sometimes in miraculous ways, or even at the moment the preacher begins preaching.

---

27. *Autobiography* 2.189.
28. *Lectures* 1.97.
29. *Lectures* 1.97.
30. *Lectures* 1.96.
31. *Lectures* 4.2.

Sermon Execution

In addition to giving the preacher the content of the sermon, Spurgeon believed that the Holy Spirit empowered the preaching event. In his lecture entitled "The Holy Spirit in Connection with Our Ministry," Spurgeon urged, "We need the Spirit of God to open our mouths that we may show forth the praises of the Lord, or else we shall not speak with power."[32] He had recognised this need in his own preaching ministry. On June 17, 1855, preaching at New Park Street Chapel, Spurgeon prayed, "It is concerning the power of the Holy Ghost that I shall speak this morning; and may you have a practical exemplification of that attribute in your own hearts, when you shall feel that the influence of the Holy Ghost is being poured out upon me, so that I am speaking the words of the living God to your souls."[33] Without the Spirit working in the sermon, Spurgeon believed preaching would remain powerless.

Spurgeon urged his students to depend on the Holy Spirit in every moment of the preaching act. He described, "The Spirit of God acts also as an *anointing oil*, and this relates to *the entire delivery*—not to the utterance merely from the mouth, but to the whole delivery of this discourse."[34] The Spirit gives the words of the sermon, empowers the act of preaching, and even guards the preacher's thoughts in order to "maintain in us a devotional frame of mind whilst we are discoursing."[35]

Ultimately, according to Spurgeon, the Holy Spirit was the only source of true power in preaching. In his September 5, 1886 sermon entitled "The Abiding of the Spirit the Glory of the Church," Spurgeon asserted, "It were better to speak six words in the power of the Holy Ghost than to preach seventy years of sermons without the Spirit."[36] Spurgeon recognised that the Holy Spirit himself empowered the full act of preaching so that it might be effective for the Spirit's purposes in the church.

---

32. *Lectures* 2.8.
33. *NPSP* 1.229.
34. *Lectures* 2.9.
35. *Lectures* 2.10.
36. *MTP* 32.487.

Sermon Application

Lastly, Spurgeon believed that the Holy Spirit was responsible for applying the truths of the sermon to the hearts and minds of the listeners. Spurgeon's aim in preaching was to communicate the gospel in such a way that the common person could understand. While he believed that it was ultimately the work of the Holy Spirit to enable a hearer to understand, he implemented practical strategies to make his sermons clearer, such as utilizing basic illustrations. And, he thought the usefulness of a sermon illustration could be judged by its effectiveness on children, an approach he learned from Alexander Fletcher.

Fletcher was a Scottish Congregationalist pastor who ministered at a church in London, officiated Charles and Susannah's wedding ceremony, and was a father-like figure to Spurgeon. A letter from November 16, 1855, captured the warmth between the aged pastor and the young preacher, as Fletcher wrote to Spurgeon, "Dear Young Brother, What a delightful, exciting, encouraging meeting we had last Thursday week in your hallowed sanctuary! The smile of God abundantly rested upon us. It was like heaven below. Truly, it *was* good to be there!"[37] Not long after Spurgeon came to London to begin his preaching ministry, he was invited to preach at Surrey Chapel, the church whose founding pastor was Rowland Hill. Spurgeon's opportunity to preach there was the first of a double fulfillment of Knill's prophetic word to the boy Spurgeon at Stambourne.[38] The opportunity arose to preach at Surrey Chapel when Fletcher, who was scheduled to give the annual children's sermon, was taken ill and had to find a replacement preacher on short notice. He asked Spurgeon to preach in his stead.

Fletcher was known for his children's sermons, and for his illustrations, and one of the lessons Spurgeon learned from Fletcher was the importance of illustrating a sermon. Spurgeon often conveyed Fletcher's wisdom: "I remember hearing Dr. Alexander Fletcher, when speaking to children, tell them a simple

---

37. *Autobiography* 4.141.

38. For more information on Knill's prophecy, see *Autobiography* 1.33–38.

anecdote in order to illustrate the joy of a man when he gets delivered from sin."[39] Spurgeon took Fletcher's lesson to heart and determined to preach in a way that the common person could comprehend the gospel.

Nevertheless, Spurgeon believed that, no matter how well a preacher did in communicating the gospel, the Holy Spirit was the only one who could effectively apply the truths of a sermon to a person's mind and heart. Two days after the 1855 Fletcher letter, Spurgeon preached a sermon in which he celebrated the conversion of a man "considered to be what the people in his neighbourhood called 'daft.'"[40] That man, who had been illiterate, was converted and became determined to learn to read so that he could read the Bible for himself. Eventually his speech developed into a modest ability for public speaking, he read a few more books, and he became "a useful minister, settled in a country village, laboring for God."[41] This exemplified, for Spurgeon, the fact that "God the Holy Spirit can teach any one, however illiterate, however uninstructed."[42] Spurgeon understood that the Holy Spirit could effectively apply the message of a sermon to any person, regardless of one's intellectual abilities.

Spurgeon's desire was to make the Scriptures known to all people, but he knew the Holy Spirit was the only one who could accomplish the task. He once recalled, "My grandfather said to me, many years ago, concerning the preparation of a sermon, and I have always remembered his words, 'I study my sermon as much as if the work of preaching depended entirely upon myself; and I go into the pulpit relying upon the Spirit of God, knowing that it does not depend upon myself, but upon him.'"[43] Only the Holy Spirit has the power to apply successfully the content of a sermon.

Ultimately, Spurgeon believed that the highest use of the sermon was to call men and women to faith in Jesus Christ, and the success of that call relied solely on the Holy Spirit. Spurgeon's

---

39. *MTP* 53.417.
40. *NPSP* 1.386.
41. *NPSP* 1.386.
42. *NPSP* 1.386.
43. *MTP* 44.110.

own conversion was the prime example as he considered the Spirit's role in applying the message of a sermon to each person. The sermon text from his conversion was Isaiah 45:22, and the simple message the Spirit used to convert him was, "Look to Jesus Christ... look and live."[44] This theme permeated Spurgeon's preaching. He often referenced the passage, and used the language of "looking to Christ" for salvation as a common call in his sermons.[45]

Spurgeon knew that for a person to see the truth about Jesus Christ from a sermon, the Holy Spirit must work effectively to give insight. For example, in his sermon on Isaiah 45:22 entitled "Life for a Look," Spurgeon exhorted, "May God the Holy Spirit enable thee thus to look to Christ; for, looking to him, as surely as he liveth, thou too shalt live; and, as surely as God is true, thou shalt be saved."[46] As he described in that sermon, a person is saved by looking to Jesus, and a person is enabled to look to Jesus by the Holy Spirit.

Conclusion

Spurgeon believed that preaching was the primary means through which the Spirit accomplished his work in the Christian and the church. As the sword of the Spirit, every aspect of preaching required the work of the Holy Spirit—the Spirit provided the content of the sermon to the preacher, empowered the preaching event, and applied the truths preached to the minds and hearts of the listeners. As Spurgeon exhorted, "See, again, the importance of preaching, for the Spirit of God descends only to help the preacher. And then see, last of all, the all-importance of the Holy Ghost. Without Him we cannot preach, we cannot hear so as to believe and be saved."[47]

---

44. *Autobiography* 1.106.

45. While the phrase, theme, or language of looking to Jesus Christ for salvation was common in Spurgeon's sermons, examples of sermons where this theme was primary include *NPSP* 2, sermon 49; *NPSP* 2, sermon 60; *NPSP* 3, sermon 153; *NPSP* 4, sermon 195; *NPSP* 7, sermon 361; *MTP* 10, sermon 575; *MTP* 13, sermon 771; *MTP* 17, sermon 968; *MTP* 34, sermon 2058; *MTP* 48, sermon 2805; and *MTP* 62, sermon 3509.

46. *MTP* 48.551.

47. *MTP* 9.300.

After publishing a sermon a week for twenty years, in January 1875 Spurgeon celebrated these twelve-hundred printed sermons, which had been translated into a number of languages and distributed to cities and towns throughout the world. He praised the Lord for the hundreds of people who indicated that they came to faith in Jesus Christ through the reading of a sermon. As he thanked God for such gracious and miraculous work through this ministry, he could not help but recognise how glorious a calling it was to preach the gospel. Spurgeon's description captured perfectly the beauty and power that he ascribed to the task of preaching:

> It is a bath in the waters of Paradise to preach with the Holy Ghost sent down from heaven. Scarcely is it possible for a man, this side of the grave, to be nearer heaven than is a preacher when his Master's presence bears him right away from every care and thought, save the one business in hand, and that the greatest that ever occupied a creature's mind and heart. No tongue can tell the amount of happiness I have enjoyed in delivering these twenty years of sermons.[48]

---

48. *S&T* 11.8.

15

"An Invisible Arm"
The Holy Spirit and Evangelism

The Holy Ghost sent down from heaven anoints all true evangelists, and is the true power and fire. The more we believe in the presence and power of the Holy Ghost, the more likely shall we be to see the Gospel triumphant in our ministry.... [T]he Gospel itself would make no progress were it not for the divine power. There is an invisible arm which pushes forward the conquests of the truth, there is a fire unfed of human fuel, which burns a way for the truth of Jesus Christ into the hearts of men.[1]

After his conversion, the first way that Spurgeon gave himself in service to his new Master was through evangelism. The transformation in his own heart sparked in Spurgeon a pastoral concern for others. With youthful exuberance he distributed tracts and evangelised door-to-door. He also selected specific tracts to mail as personal correspondences to friends and acquaintances in hopes that the personal relationship might aid in their coming to faith in Jesus. As a follow-up to his distribution of tracts, he gave his Saturdays to visiting with those who were interested in hearing more about the gospel.

Spurgeon's conversion also generated a special concern for the spiritual life of his siblings. In June of 1850, Spurgeon wrote to his mother after hearing that his sister Sarah professed faith in Jesus Christ. He celebrated, "I am so glad that Sarah, too, is called, that two of us in one household at one time should thus openly profess

---

1. *MTP* 15.75–76.

the Saviour's name."[2] Similarly, in December of the same year, Spurgeon wrote to his sister Louisa, lovingly cheered her for her wonderful name, and then encouraged, "If anyone is called by the name of Christian, that is better than all these great [names]: it is the best name in the world, except the name of our Lord Jesus Christ."[3] Whether with strangers or his family, Spurgeon's Christian life began with an excitement for evangelism.

Evangelism and Pastoral Ministry

As a pastor, Spurgeon continued to prioritise sharing the gospel. The church followed their pastor's example, and this evangelistic fervor became a defining mark of the church's shared ministry. Eighteen years into his pastoral tenure in London, Spurgeon continued to exhort his church to share the gospel and call others to faith in Christ. He was clear that the success of their evangelism would not be found with clever or eloquent speech; rather, as Spurgeon declared, "At this moment the only vindication of our existence is the presence and work of the Paraclete among us."[4] After nearly two decades of work, Spurgeon recalled the negativity he faced, often being "under much opposition and hostile criticism," and his preaching "being condemned on all hands as vulgar, unlearned, and, in fact, a nine days' wonder."[5] Nevertheless, he celebrated that while "Many other pulpits were intellectual... we were Puritanical."[6] Whereas "Rhetorical essays were the wares retailed by most of the preachers... we gave the people the gospel, we brought out before the world the old Reformers' doctrines, Calvinistic truth, Augustinian teaching, and Pauline dogma."[7] One "wiseacre," as Spurgeon facetiously called him, referred to Spurgeon's ministry as the "echo of an exploded evangelism."[8] Spurgeon was more than happy that

---

2. *Letters* 24.
3. *Letters* 68.
4. *MTP* 18.558–59.
5. *MTP* 18.559.
6. *MTP* 18.559.
7. *MTP* 18.559.
8. *MTP* 18.559.

the church's ministry would be associated with an evangelism explosion. Even more, he was happy to admit that the force behind the explosion was not "comeliness of words" or "polished speech," but was "the power of the Spirit of God to keep on preaching Christ and glorifying the Saviour."[9] For Spurgeon, the church's evangelism was the reverberation from an explosion of the Spirit's power, and this evangelistic explosion became the defining mark of his ministry.

There are numerous examples of men and women coming to faith through the ministry of New Park Street Chapel and the Metropolitan Tabernacle. Through Spurgeon's evangelistic preaching, the witness of deacons or elders, or the testimony of members of the church, men and women came to faith in Jesus Christ from all different backgrounds: wealthy and poor, working class and culturally elite, atheists and worldly, those who grew up in a Christian home and those who had ungodly parents, sick, healthy, successful, downtrodden, and everywhere in between.

One such example was of a man named James Kirkwood. An elder at the church, Thomas Moor, wrote about Kirkwood: "I believe the Spirit's mighty work is evident in this man— convictions deep, tears many, prayers earnest and melting, peace groaningly sought for, and holy joy at last by believing in Christ."[10] Even in his coming to Christ, Kirkwood struggled to understand and believe the doctrines of graces. Over weeks of intentional and collective discipleship Moor provided pastoral insight, reading materials, and an invitation to a Sunday School class; a faithful Christian friend offered Kirkwood personal counsel; and Spurgeon's sermons provided biblical guidance. Over time, Kirkwood was led to affirm the doctrine of election as biblically revealed, and even "to rejoice in that doctrine as one that exalts the wisdom and love of God."[11]

---

9. *MTP* 18.559.

10. Hannah Wyncoll, *Wonders of Grace: Original Testimonies of Converts During Spurgeon's Early Years* (London: The Wakeman Trust, 2016), 87.

11. Wyncoll, 88.

Evangelism, the Spirit, and Prayer

The stories of those who came to faith in Jesus through the ministry of the church are a testament to the collective efforts of Christians who individually were empowered to share the gospel. Through his pastoral leadership, Spurgeon continually called all Christians to participate in evangelistic ministry. As encouraged as he was about the ministry of their church, he also spoke very strongly in urging for greater effort by all Christians to evangelise. In April 1856, he preached a sermon on behalf of the Baptist Missionary Society in which he exhorted, "Ah! there ought to be more of us who are preaching to the heathen, and yet, perhaps, we are indolent and doing little or nothing. There are many of you, yea all of you, who ought to be doing far more than you are for evangelical purposes and the spread of Christ's gospel."[12] Spurgeon provoked an urgency to evangelise, and to do so liberally. Considering that "sudden bereavements may come," Spurgeon urged, "Oh, my brothers and sisters in Christ, if sinners will be damned, at least let them leap to hell over our bodies; and if they will perish, let them perish with our arms about their knees, imploring them to stay, and not madly to destroy themselves. If hell must be filled, at least let it be filled in the teeth of our exertions, and let not one go there unwarned and unprayed for."[13] Spurgeon desired that all Christians should venture to tell all people the gospel of Jesus Christ.

Even with his urging for evangelism, Spurgeon believed that effectiveness in sharing the gospel was directly attributed to the Holy Spirit from beginning to end. The first step in evangelism was for the Holy Spirit to create the desire in the Christian to share the gospel. No matter how earnest his preaching, Spurgeon believed that the Spirit must be the one to compel the Christian to evangelise. On January 7, 1877, Spurgeon preached on the "Urgent Need of the Holy Spirit." In the introduction to the sermon he described that within the church there "must be a manifestation of the power of the Holy Spirit," and in order to "invade the

12. *NPSP* 2.184.
13. *MTP* 7.11.

territories of the enemy and... conquer the world for Christ [the church] must be clothed with the selfsame sacred energy."[14] The Holy Spirit's first work in evangelism was to stir up in the hearts of Christians a desire for Christ and the Scriptures. As Spurgeon concluded, "Only let the church be illuminated by the Holy Spirit and she will reflect the light and become to onlookers 'fair as the moon, clear as the sun, and terrible as an army with banners.'"[15]

Then, Spurgeon believed that as Christians shared the gospel the Holy Spirit must empower their evangelistic work in order for it to be effective. Spurgeon knew that without the Spirit evangelism would remain fruitless. However, when empowered by the Holy Spirit, there was no limit to the success of Christian evangelism. Spurgeon urged, "In all the acts of the Christian's life ... the Christian finds his weakness and his powerlessness, unless he is clothed about with the Spirit of God."[16] "Here is this England of ours," Spurgeon described, "sunk in stolid ignorance of the gospel."[17] As the Christian searched for more ways to call people to faith in Jesus Christ, Spurgeon stipulated, "Do not say that we want money.... Do not say that we want buildings, churches, edifices; all these may be very well in subserviency.... The one thing then which we want, is the Spirit of God."[18] As Christians proclaim the gospel "the Spirit touches men's hearts" and they are led to faith in Jesus Christ.[19] Spurgeon taught that success in evangelism required the Spirit's work to empower the evangelist and cause the heart of the hearer to believe.

Lastly, given the necessity of the Holy Spirit in evangelism, Spurgeon believed that the undergirding work of evangelism was prayer. In his June 12, 1864 sermon on John 16:7, one phrase summarised Spurgeon's message: "where the Spirit of God is there is liberty and power."[20] This was a line that Spurgeon repeated in

---

14. *MTP* 23.13.
15. *MTP* 23.13.
16. *NPSP* 5.215.
17. *MTP* 10.337.
18. *MTP* 10.337.
19. *MTP* 10.337.
20. *MTP* 10.339.

his sermons. Twenty-three years later, preaching on the necessity of the Holy Spirit for the church's ministry, Spurgeon again proclaimed, "Where the Spirit of God is, there is power."[21]

In his first use of the phrase, Spurgeon called the church to "wake up... to earnest prayer."[22] Since the church's evangelism could only be accomplished in the Spirit's power, Spurgeon exhorted the church to pray, "Lord, send the Spirit! Send the Spirit, Lord! Work! Work! Work!"[23] Without the presence and power of the Holy Spirit, the evangelistic work of the church would return void. Therefore, as Spurgeon described, "I am persuaded we only want more prayer, and there is no limit to the blessing; you may evangelize England, you may evangelize Europe, you may Christianize the world, if ye do but know how to pray."[24] Spurgeon urged the church to give the Lord "no rest till he sendeth forth his Spirit once again to stir the waters, and to brood over this dark world till light and life shall come."[25] In order for the church to experience power in their evangelistic ministry, the primary activity of the Christian must be to pray for the Spirit to move in power.

Conclusion

Spurgeon believed that the Holy Spirit worked through the church's evangelism as an essential means of bringing people to faith in Jesus Christ. Simply put, Spurgeon understood evangelism as proclaiming the truth of Christ and calling people to believe. Soon after his own conversion Spurgeon personally shared the gospel, and as a pastor he prioritised the church's need to share the gospel. Thus, his ministry was defined by an evangelistic fervor.

Moreover, the Holy Spirit was vital to the effectiveness of the church's evangelism. Human ability alone is insufficient to bring a person to faith; therefore, both the act of evangelism and

21. *MTP* 33.146.
22. *MTP* 10.339.
23. *MTP* 10.340.
24. *MTP* 10.340.
25. *MTP* 10.340.

a response in faith required the supernatural power of the Holy Spirit. For Spurgeon, the Spirit created the desire in Christians to share the gospel, empowered the evangelistic act, and caused the hearer to believe. Given the necessity of the Spirit's work in evangelism, Spurgeon believed the most basic evangelistic work of the church was prayer. Spurgeon's call, then, to the church was to pray for the Spirit's power and participate in the work of evangelism. As Spurgeon declared, "if there were the might of the Spirit attending them, the humblest evangelists would be more successful than the most pompous of divines, or the most eloquent of preachers."[26] Indeed, the Holy Spirit is the "invisible arm [of God] which pushes forward the conquests of the truth."[27]

26. *NPSP* 2.183.

27. *MTP* 15.76.

16

"The Great Householder"
The Holy Spirit and His Gifts

There are many kinds of gifts. All Christians have some gift.
Some may have but one talent, but all have one at the least. The
Great Householder has apportioned to every servant a talent....
O Spirit of the living God, lead all thy people to downright,
earnest, and actual service of the Redeemer, and especially work
in us to that end.[1]

While there was a temptation among some Christians in the
nineteenth century to focus too much on spiritual gifts,
Spurgeon felt that the greater danger of the church in his time
was too little attention given to the gifts of the Spirit. He was
concerned that many churches were growing cold to the Spirit's
work. In his 1862 sermon on John 16:14, he lamented, "Just now
we are in little danger from the excesses of fevered brains, for,
as a rule, our sin is in being far too cold and dead to spiritual
influences. I fear we are liable to another evil, and are apt to forget
the person and work of the Comforter altogether."[2]

Certainly Spurgeon wanted to avoid the danger of "running
wild with whimsies and fancies about inner lights and new
revelations." He was more afraid, however, of "this putting the
revelation above the revealer, this taking the book without the
author, this preaching of the truth without the great truth-applyer,
this going forth to work with the sword, forgetting that it is the

---

1. *MTP* 18.633, 792.
2. *MTP* 8.459.

sword of the Spirit, and only mighty as the Holy Ghost maketh it 'mighty to the pulling down of strongholds.'"[3]

Spurgeon knew that unless Christians were faithful to use their own spiritual gifts, their ministry would soon die. So, he prayed, "May this Church ever continue to reverence the Holy Spirit without exaggerating his work! May we prize him, love him, and adore him."[4]

Spurgeon recognised that there were both natural and spiritual gifts. All people possessed the former, but the latter were a unique blessing of the Holy Spirit to Christians. As Spurgeon explained, Christians "may expect the Spirit of God to bestow upon us, gifts which can be used in the Church of Christ, and which we desire to possess in order that we may use them to the glory of God."[5] The way the Holy Spirit puts Christians to use for the church is by giving gifts, and, according to Spurgeon, the Spirit gives gifts to all Christians for the purposes of building up the church, witnessing to the world, and glorifying God.

Spurgeon believed that all the gifts listed in Ephesians 4:11 and 1 Corinthians 12:7–11 were active in the church, though they were active in the church at various times according to the Spirit's will. In his exposition of Ephesians 4, Spurgeon indicated that those particular gifts were present in the church at the appropriate time and based on the Spirit's discernment. He explained, "The early Church could not have been without apostles, and we cannot do without evangelists."[6] Likewise, while he affirmed the validity of the spiritual gifts listed in 1 Corinthians 12, he was uncertain whether they all continued to be present in the church.

In addition to these two biblical lists, Spurgeon also assumed a variety of other spiritual gifts. For example, in his sermon "Our Gifts and How to Use Them," he included the gifts of influence, speaking, writing, experience, prayer, and conversation. Overall,

---

3. *MTP* 8.459.

4. *MTP* 8.459.

5. *MTP* 46.458.

6. *MTP* 40.562.

Spurgeon conveyed, "There are many kinds of gifts. All Christians have some gift."[7]

Moreover, preaching on Ephesians 4 Spurgeon explained the purpose of spiritual gifts: "The spiritual gifts of the church are for the good of the rebels as well as for the building up of those who are reconciled. Sinner, every true minister exists for thy good, and all the workers of the church have an eye to you."[8]

In 1881, Spurgeon recognised that a significant number of new people had become part of the church, and pastorally he aimed to help them see that their spiritual gifts were intended to build up the church and for use in the service of Jesus Christ. He began his September 1, 1881, sermon by addressing the new members: "Dear friend, now that you have become a member of a Christian church, you should say to yourself, 'What can I do for it?'"[9] He elaborated, "Every one of us should pray that he may have as much to use for Christ as he can use, and that he may be as well fitted by the Holy Spirit for the Master's service as it is possible that he can be."[10]

The Miraculous Gifts

Spurgeon was uncertain whether the miraculous gifts, such as healing, working miracles, and speaking in tongues, continued to exist in the church. Although he did not observe these miraculous gifts at use in the church, he also did not reject the possibility of the Spirit to operate in miraculous ways. In 1856, preaching on Hebrews 6:4–6, Spurgeon made a passing comment on the nature of the miraculous gifts in his time. He argued that the people referred to in the text must be Christians, since they had received "all those powers with which the Holy Ghost endows a Christian."[11] Spurgeon clarified that this phrase did not indicate "miraculous gifts," because those were "denied us in these

---

7. *MTP* 18.633.
8. *MTP* 17.180.
9. *MTP* 46.457.
10. *MTP* 46.457.
11. *NPSP* 2.171.

days."[12] By this comment, Spurgeon indicated his belief that the miraculous gifts were no longer active.

However, later in his ministry Spurgeon indicated he was less certain whether the miraculous gifts had ceased. In his 1881 sermon on 1 Corinthians 12:31, Spurgeon confessed: "How far the gifts of healing may still remain in the Church, I should not like to be forced to say;—either to say that they remain, lest any should be led into fanaticism; or to say that they are utterly gone, lest I should be denying some things which, at any rate, look like facts."[13]

Rather than focus on the miraculous gifts, Spurgeon drew the attention of his congregation to the gifts of the Spirit in salvation, such as regeneration. As Spurgeon explained:

> Now, be it never forgotten that those works of the Holy Spirit which are permanent must assuredly be of greater value than those which were transitory.... those works of the Holy Spirit which are at this time vouchsafed to the Church of God are every way as valuable as those earlier miraculous gifts which have departed from us. The work of the Holy Spirit, by which men are quickened from their death in sin, is not inferior to the power which made men speak with tongues.[14]

While Spurgeon remained uncertain as to whether the miraculous gifts continued in the church, he was confident that the greater gifts of the Spirit were his work of regenerating, converting, sanctifying, and preserving the Christian.

Spurgeon's theological position on the continuation or cessation of the miraculous gifts was primarily influenced by his biblical and historical theology, but it was also influenced by his personal experience. The fact that Spurgeon, over the course of his life, personally experienced supernatural insights from the Holy Spirit was a significant factor in shaping his theology of the Spirit's miraculous works. One of the ways that he experienced the supernatural influence of the Holy Spirit was as a child when Richard Knill prophesied that Spurgeon would one day preach at Rowland Hill's church. This experience shaped Spurgeon's

---

12. *NPSP* 2.171.

13. *MTP* 46.458–59.

14. *MTP* 30.386.

understanding of the Spirit's sovereign work in his call to ministry. And, of course, when Spurgeon did eventually preach at that church, his belief in the continued miraculous working of the Spirit was further cemented.

After being on the receiving end of a prophetic word, Spurgeon also experienced several instances in which he gave a prophetic word from the Holy Spirit. In his *Autobiography*, he recounted services at Surrey Garden, and explained, "There were many instances of remarkable conversions at the Music Hall."[15] While he was preaching one Sunday, he pointed to a man in the crowd, whom he did not know, and said, "There is a man sitting there, who is a shoemaker; he keeps his shop open on Sundays, it was open last Sabbath morning, he took ninepence, and there was fourpence profit out of it; his soul is sold to Satan for fourpence!"[16] Later, a member of the church met a man who perfectly fitted Spurgeon's description and discovered that Spurgeon's words were totally accurate. Spurgeon noted that a dozen similar cases existed of him accurately speaking about a topic he was not informed of, to a person he did not know, only because he was "moved by the Spirit to say it."[17]

Spurgeon's biblical understanding and personal experience made him confident in the Spirit's continued ability to work in miraculous ways, yet also cautious of continually expecting these occurrences to be normative or authoritative in the Christian's life. When he reflected on these types of miraculous occurrences in his July 27, 1869, sermon entitled "A Well-Ordered Life," he indicated, "Some, I know, fall into a very vicious habit, which habit they excuse to themselves—namely, that of ordering their footsteps according to impressions."[18] Spurgeon, elaborating on his understanding of these impressions, explained: "There are occasionally impressions of the Holy Spirit which guide men where no other guidance could have answered the end."[19] As

15. *Autobiography* 2.226.
16. *Autobiography* 2.226.
17. *Autobiography* 2.227.
18. *MTP* 15.368.
19. *MTP* 15.368.

an example, he recalled the story of a Quaker who followed an impression of the Spirit to go to a particular house in the middle of the night, and, unknowingly, his knock on the door thwarted the homeowner's attempted suicide. Such occurrences were, according to Spurgeon, unexpected gifts from the Holy Spirit intended to fulfill a particular purpose. However, Christians abuse these miraculous works of the Spirit when such impressions are treated with authority that is reserved for the Scriptures alone. So, Spurgeon urged, "Not your impressions, but that which is in this [Bible] must always guide you."[20] As Spurgeon experienced firsthand, the Holy Spirit often works in miraculous ways to bless the church, but the Spirit's work in these ways is not intended to usurp the authority of the Scripture in the life of a Christian.

Conclusion

Spurgeon believed that the Holy Spirit gave spiritual gifts to Christians, and that each Christian should use his or her gifting to build up the church, and to serve as a witness for Christ in the world. Spurgeon noticed a sense of apathy in the church regarding spiritual gifts, and therefore he desired that the church in his time would focus more on the Holy Spirit, and would give specific attention to the use of the gifts that the Spirit gives to all Christians. In his biblical interpretation, Spurgeon was uncertain whether the miraculous gifts of the Spirit were all still present in the church. However, from personal experience, he maintained that the Spirit continued to work in miraculous ways. As Spurgeon expressed, from his exposition on 1 Corinthians 12,

> Whatever our gifts as a church, or as individuals, may be, they all come from the selfsame Spirit.... Let us all trace whatever gift we have to the hand that gave it, and to the Spirit that wrought it; let us feel that we are so many pipes connected with one fountain; and, therefore, as all the good that we convey comes from the one source, let us give all the honour and glory of it to the Spirit of God from whom it comes.[21]

---

20. *MTP* 15.368.
21. *MTP* 47.406.

Conclusion
The Spirit of God Like the Soft South Wind

> Remember, however, that *the best Quickener is always the Holy Spirit;* and that blessed Spirit can come as the north wind, convincing us of sin, and tearing away every rag of our self-confidence, or he may come as the soft south wind, all full of love, revealing Christ, and the covenant of grace, and all the blessings treasured for us therein. Come, Holy Spirit! Come as the Heavenly Dove, or as the rushing mighty wind; but do come![1]

In the summer of 1848, another cholera outbreak ravished London, this time concentrated on the southern banks of the River Thames.[2] As a modern epidemiologist described, "During the 1848–9 cholera outbreak some of the highest mortality rates in the country were located in London's south bank areas of Lambeth and Southwark."[3] After a brief respite the disease struck again in 1853, followed by another violent episode in 1854. Finally, Dr. John Snow, later called the father of modern epidemiology, determined that the source of the outbreak was the water from the Broad Street water pump in the Soho district of London.[4] Snow's water pump sat four miles northwest of Spurgeon's New Park Street Chapel, just across the River Thames. Spurgeon, nineteen years old and in the first year of his pastoral ministry

---

1. *MTP* 42.354 (emphasis added).

2. Amanda J. Thomas, *Cholera: The Victorian Plague* (Barnsley: Pen & Sword History, 2015), 129–61.

3. Ibid., 137–38.

4. For more on Snow as the father of modern epidemiology, see Ilona Carneiro and Natasha Howard, *Introduction to Epidemiology*, 2nd ed. (Maidenhead: Open University Press, 2011), 10. For more on the source of the outbreak, see Thomas, *Cholera*, 138–39.

among the Southwark congregation, became overwhelmed with the constancy of death among his parishioners. He later reflected on the event:

> In the year 1854, when I had scarcely been in London twelve months, the neighbourhood in which I laboured was visited by Asiatic cholera, and my congregation suffered from its inroads. Family after family summoned me to the bedside of the smitten, and almost every day I was called to visit the grave. I gave myself up with youthful ardour to the visitation of the sick, and was sent for from all corners of the district by persons of all ranks and religions. I became weary in body and sick at heart.[5]

As Dr. Snow searched for the cause of the outbreak, Spurgeon searched for something "with the power to soothe the heart."[6] He came across the words of Psalm 91:9–10 handwritten in bold lettering on the window of a shoemaker's store: "Because thou hast made the Lord, which is my refuge, even the Most High, thy habitation; there shall no evil befall thee, neither shall any plague come nigh thy dwelling."[7] Spurgeon believed that finding these verses written on that window was as much a work of the Holy Spirit in his life as the inspiration of the text in Scripture. Later, when Spurgeon wrote his commentary on the passage, he described that in 1854 the words of Psalm 91 became like aloe to his wearied soul once they were "applied by the Holy Spirit."[8] This experience from early in his ministry proved to Spurgeon how desperately he must depend on the Holy Spirit in his life and ministry. From then on, the great preacher overflowed with teaching on the person and work of the Holy Spirit.

The Spirit Like the South Wind

To teach on the person and work of the Holy Spirit, Spurgeon often employed the biblical metaphor relating the Holy Spirit to the wind. Specifically, Spurgeon frequently compared the work of

---

5. *TD* 4.235.
6. *TD* 4.235.
7. *Autobiography* 1.403.
8. *Autobiography* 1.403.

the Holy Spirit to the "south wind." The natural weather patterns in both the Ancient Near East (context of the Old Testament) and the Mediterranean world (context of the New Testament), which were each consistent with Spurgeon's own geographical context, were the foundation of Spurgeon's south wind imagery. His sermon on January 14, 1866, entitled "Frost and Thaw," set the stage for his use of this metaphor as Spurgeon laid out the pattern of the winds affecting London.

The first part of the "Frost and Thaw" sermon focused on God's divine operations over nature. Just as God brings snow and ice, he also causes the snow and ice to melt by bringing the warm south wind. Whether the wind "comes from the north to freeze, or from the south to melt, it is [God's] wind."[9] Likewise, preaching on Luke 12:54–57, Spurgeon observed that "a cloud in the western sky betokened rain, and a wind from the south was the sign of heat."[10] Along with the natural easternly moving wind pattern, Spurgeon recognised that winds from the north brought cold air and winds from the south brought warmth.

With a proper understanding of the typical wind patterns as his foundation, Spurgeon then spiritualised his use of the south wind imagery to describe the work of the Holy Spirit. In the "Frost and Thaw" sermon, Spurgeon employed the imagery to illustrate how the Spirit gives life to God's people just as the south wind brings the fruition of spring: "the sweet breath of the Holy Spirit like the warm south wind blows, then the waters flow and the heart is filled with holy joy, and light, and liberty, for God is there."[11] Again, in his July 9, 1882 sermon, Spurgeon explained, "Softly and gently works the Holy Spirit, even as the breath of spring which dissolves the iceberg and melts the glacier.... the soft south wind blows, and all is life and liberty."[12] While Spurgeon did not neglect the painful work of the Spirit's conviction, which operated like the cold north wind, he celebrated that the Spirit ultimately brings vitality to the Christian, like the life-giving

---

9. *MTP* 12.26.
10. *MTP* 19.553.
11. *MTP* 12.31.
12. *MTP* 28.378.

south wind. In all, Spurgeon described the work of the Spirit, like the south wind, as fructifying, edifying, liberating, energizing, satisfying, melting, sweet, soft, warm, gentle, and balmy, bringing love, freedom, faith, song, joy, peace, and hope.

Spurgeon also included the south wind imagery in his personal correspondences. In the spring of 1871, illness and fatigue caused him to be absent from his congregation for more than a dozen Sundays in a row. On the day before his thirty-seventh birthday, he issued a letter that was read to the congregation during the Sunday service. He began the letter by explaining how the change in the weather had helped to improve his health, as it "pleased God to turn the wind at the beginning of this week, and the change in the temperature has worked wonders."[13] He thanked his congregation for their prayers for him, and indicated his intent to return to preaching in two weeks. At the conclusion of the letter, thinking of the wind system that had brought warmth and healing to his physical body, Spurgeon expressed, "May the soft south wind of the Spirit's love be among you, and may you pour forth praise as flowers breathe perfume."[14]

Similarly, three years later Spurgeon wrote a letter from Mentone to his "Young Friends" in the church.[15] He encouraged them for their faithful attendance, and reminded them of the work of Jesus Christ as redeemer. Spurgeon juxtaposed the current fog and rain in London with the flowers and summer weather in Mentone, and used the contrasting weather conditions as an illustration for "the change which faith makes in the soul."[16] Considering the warm winds on the southern coast of France, Spurgeon prayed, "May the Spirit of God, like the soft south wind, breathe upon you, and make your hearts bloom with desires, blossom with hopes, and bring forth fruits of repentance!"[17] Through both his sermons and personal communications, Spurgeon utilised the south wind

13. *MTP* 17.336.
14. *MTP* 17.336.
15. *Letters* 176.
16. *Letters* 176.
17. *Letters* 176.

imagery to illustrate the necessary and life-giving work of the Holy Spirit.

This south wind imagery, as seen in Spurgeon's sermons and letters, exhibited five characteristic themes of his theology of the Holy Spirit. First, Spurgeon used this metaphor to indicate that the Holy Spirit was a divine person of God. Just as the wind moved according to the will of God, so too the Holy Spirit operated as a person with a will, not as an impersonal force. As Spurgeon explained in his July 1882 use of the south wind imagery, the Holy Spirit "comes according to his own sovereign pleasure."[18] In that context, Spurgeon intentionally used the pronoun "his" instead of "its" in order to highlight the personhood of the Holy Spirit. In his May 1887 sermon titled "The Heavenly Wind," Spurgeon used the metaphor to argue:

> No proclamation nor purpose under heaven will be able to affect the wind by so much as half a point of the compass. It will blow according to its own sweet will, where it pleases, when it pleases, how it pleases, and as it pleases.… So is it, only in a far higher and more emphatic sense, with the Holy Spirit, for he is most free and absolute.… he is God himself, and absolutely free.[19]

In his use of the south wind metaphor, Spurgeon maintained the deity and personhood of the Spirit.

Second, Spurgeon believed that the Holy Spirit was the efficacious agent of God who empowered all of God's work in the world. Even as the wind was the effective power of the weather, so the Holy Spirit was the agent of God operating in the world. The Spirit enabled the creation event, hovered over the created mass to bring order, breathed life into human beings, dictated Scripture, empowered the birth and ministry of Jesus Christ, and applied the blessings of God to the Christian. In Spurgeon's one hundred and fifth sermon, preaching from Ephesians 6:17 on the Spirit's work in Scripture, he conveyed, "The Spirit is the great executive. He dictated the words of the glorious Trinity."[20]

18. *MTP* 28.378.
19. *MTP* 23.303–04.
20. *LS* 2.41.

In the same way that the Spirit was the executive agent of the Triune God in creating Scripture, so also the Spirit, like the wind, empowered every action of God in the world.

Third, through his use of the south wind metaphor Spurgeon attributed ministry success to the Holy Spirit. Spurgeon's ministry was centred on preaching Christ and calling men and women to believe in Jesus and receive new life. Nonetheless, he believed that his preaching would remain ineffective if the Holy Spirit did not empower it, and that new life could only be given to a person by the direct work of the Spirit. Hence, Spurgeon recognised that the purpose of his ministry was fully dependent on the Holy Spirit. In January 1855, Spurgeon described that by the end of the calendar year "more than two hundred thousand of my productions will be scattered through the land—words uttered by my lips, or written by my pen."[21] However, he believed that the only way these writings would be useful for God's purposes was "by incessant prayer for the Holy Spirit; by constantly calling down the influence of the Holy Ghost upon us… that he would come and own our labors, that the whole church at large may be revived thereby, and not ourselves only, but the whole world share in the benefit."[22]

At the end of his May 15, 1890 sermon, Spurgeon built on the south wind imagery and urged that the Holy Spirit "can come unexpectedly upon you in the pew during these five minutes that remain. You are perhaps thinking about whether you can catch an early train, and get home. May the Holy Spirit lay hold of you before you leave the building, and get you home in real earnest to your God and to your Father!"[23] Just as the wind was necessary for human life to exist, Spurgeon believed that the Spirit was essential for giving new life to the Christian. Thus, he credited all ministry success to the person and work of the Holy Spirit.

Fourth, Spurgeon argued that the sweetness of the south wind was comparable to the sweetness in the Holy Spirit's work in bringing the Christian into fellowship with Jesus Christ. This

21.   *NPSP* 1.32.

22.   *NPSP* 1.32.

23.   *MTP* 38.120.

work of the Spirit exemplified how Spurgeon's Christology and pneumatology were intimately related. In his October 9, 1859, sermon on grieving the Holy Spirit, Spurgeon explained:

> I am afraid, dear friends, we are too much in the habit of talking of the love of Jesus, without thinking of the love of the Holy Spirit. Now I would not wish to exalt one person of the Trinity above another, but I do feel this, that because Jesus Christ was a man, bone of our bone, and flesh of our flesh, and therefore there was something tangible in him that can be seen with the eyes, and handled with the hands, therefore we more readily think of him, and fix our love on him, than we do upon the Spirit.[24]

Spurgeon did not diminish his emphasis on Jesus Christ in order to exalt the Holy Spirit. Rather, he urged, "Let us love Jesus with all our hearts, and let us love the Holy Spirit too. Let us have songs for him, gratitude for him. We do not forget Christ's cross, let us not forget the Spirit's operations. We do not forget what Jesus has done for us, let us always remember what the Spirit does in us."[25] In his exposition of Song of Solomon 4, Spurgeon described that the Spirit provided the Christian with "blessed and hallowed fellowship with her Lord."[26] He maintained that communion with Christ was the root of all blessedness, and that the Spirit alone created this communion. Thus, in his 1874 letter to his "Young Friends," Spurgeon described the necessity of the Holy Spirit for a relationship with Christ: "From Jesus [the Holy Spirit] proceeds, and to Jesus He leads the soul. Look to Him. Oh, look to Him; to Him alone; to Him simply; to Him at once!"[27] Through his use of the south wind metaphor, Spurgeon maintained the necessity of the work of Jesus and of the Holy Spirit for the Christian's salvation. In this way, the person and work of Christ and the person and work of the Spirit were inseparable in Spurgeon's theology.

---

24. *NPSP* 5.428.
25. *NPSP* 5.428–29.
26. *MTP* 56.516.
27. *Letters* 176.

Fifth, the blowing of the Holy Spirit like the south wind displayed the Spirit's work to regenerate, convert, sanctify, and sustain the Christian. In the introduction to his 1862 sermon on Song of Solomon 2:10–13, Spurgeon described:

> Thanks be unto God, the soft south wind breathes upon our soul, and at once the waters of desire are set free, the spring of love cometh on, flowers of hope appear in our hearts, the trees of faith put forth their young shoots, the tone of the singing of birds cometh in our hearts, and we have joy and peace in believing through the Lord Jesus Christ.[28]

Every blessing accomplished in the Christian's life, from regeneration through perseverance, can only be achieved through the work of the Holy Spirit. Hence, Spurgeon concluded the sermon by praying, "May God grant that the people who fear his name may be stirred up this morning, if not by my words, yet by the words of my text, and by the influences of God's Spirit."[29]

Spurgeon's Pneumatology: From Beginning to End

As we have seen throughout this book, Spurgeon's theology depended on the person and work of the Spirit. In fact, Spurgeon believed that even the ability to do theology required the Spirit to enlighten a person's mind. As such, the Holy Spirit himself is utterly essential to proper Christian theology, and, at the same time, a proper understanding of the Holy Spirit is also essential in order to think rightly about God. In his 1858 sermon titled "The Outpouring of the Holy Spirit," Spurgeon claimed, "The work of the Holy Spirit is the peculiar mystery of the Christian religion."[30] He was trying to express that thinking rightly about the Holy Spirit led to a proper understanding of the Christian gospel. Yet, only the Holy Spirit himself could lead the Christian into this right thinking about the Spirit.

Again, four years later, in the opening lines of his August 1862 sermon on John 16:14, Spurgeon urged:

---

28. *MTP* 8.109.
29. *MTP* 8.120.
30. *NPSP* 4.291.

We always need the Spirit of God in our preaching; but I think we more especially require his divine direction and instruction when the subject is *himself*: for the Holy Spirit is so mysterious in his varied attributes and operations, that unless he himself shall reveal himself to us, and give us the words in which to speak of him, we shall surely fail either to understand for ourselves, or to enlighten others. In *his* light we see light, but without him we grope like blind men in the dark.[31]

Spurgeon continued to emphasise the necessity of the Spirit throughout his ministry. In his May 13, 1860, sermon, Spurgeon incorporated a Trinitarian doxology, which ended with a particular focus on the Holy Spirit. That doxology encapsulated Spurgeon's emphasis on the person and work of the Holy Spirit in his preaching:

Thou, O Father, art the source of all grace, all love and mercy towards us. Thou, O Son, art the channel of thy Father's mercy, and without thee thy Father's love could never flow to us. And thou, O Spirit—thou art he who enables us to receive that divine virtue which flows from the fountain-head, the Father, through Christ the channel, and by thy means enters into our spirit, and there abides and brings forth its glorious fruit. Magnify, then, the Spirit, ye who are partakers of it; "praise, laud, and love his name always, for it is seemly so to do."[32]

Spurgeon also led his church to praise the Spirit through singing. In September of 1866, Spurgeon's publishers printed the hymnbook that Spurgeon had curated for his congregation. Hymn 451, written by Spurgeon himself, was titled "The Holy Ghost Is Here."[33] Stanzas three and four praised:

He dwells within our soul,
    An ever welcomed Guest;
He reigns with absolute control,
    As Monarch in the breast.

---

31. *MTP* 8.457.

32. *NPSP* 6.229.

33. *Hymnbook* 451.

Our bodies are His shrine,
  And He th' indwelling Lord;
All hail, thou Comforter divine,
  Be evermore adored.[34]

Spurgeon believed the Holy Spirit was the "Lord of life," and, as in his preaching, he led his church to praise the Spirit through singing.[35]

Spurgeon also extended the same emphasis on the necessity of the Spirit in training his pastoral students for ministry. In 1872, Spurgeon delivered the presidential address at the Pastor's College conference, and in the first point of his message he exhorted, "We unfeignedly believe in [the Holy Spirit's] Deity and personality. We speak of His influences, because He has influences, but we do not forget that He is a Person from whom those influences stream; we believe in His offices, for He has offices, but we rejoice in the Person who fills them, and makes them effectual for our good."[36] In his ministry, Spurgeon preached on the person and work of the Spirit, praised the Spirit through singing, and instructed his pastoral students on the necessity of the Spirit's work.

The Legacy of Spurgeon's Ministry

The legacy of Spurgeon's ministry was his call for all people to hope in Jesus Christ. In that desire, he depended completely on the Holy Spirit to give the faith and life that is promised to the one believing in Jesus. After Spurgeon's death at Mentone, those who knew him celebrated his life and reflected on the blessed magnitude of his ministry. His publishers printed the announcement: "It is with profound regret that the Publishers record the death of the beloved Pastor of the Metropolitan Tabernacle. He was called to his rest, at Mentone, on Sunday, January 31st, at 11 p.m."[37]

The following week, Sunday, February 14, Susannah selected for print the sermon her husband had preached at the funeral of his

34. *Hymnbook* 451.
35. *Hymnbook* 451.
36. *AARM* 6–7.
37. *MTP* 38.72.

friend William Olney. As the publishers described, Susannah felt "that her dear husband could not have delivered a more suitable discourse for 'his own funeral sermon.' She has, therefore, given it that title in the hope that many will be blessed by the message which 'he, being dead, yet speaketh.'"[38] In that sermon, Spurgeon began by affirming the resurrection of Jesus Christ from the dead as prophesied and empowered by the Holy Spirit, so that "he that believeth in [Jesus Christ], though he were dead, yet shall he live, and live for ever with his risen, reigning Redeemer."[39]

For a person to believe this gospel and maintain that belief throughout life, one must "begin with God's Word, and pray God the Holy Ghost to reveal it to you till you really know it."[40] Spurgeon called men and women to believe in Jesus Christ, knowing that only the Holy Spirit could lead a person to faith, and secure for him or her life after death. The legacy of Spurgeon's pastoral ministry emphasised faith in Jesus Christ and dependence on the Holy Spirit.

As for himself, Spurgeon found true hope on a wintry morning in early January 1850, and he found true peace on a quiet evening in late January 1892. It was on a Sunday morning that a young wanderer's eyes were opened to new life as he looked to Christ, and it was on a Sunday evening that the great preacher opened his eyes in eternal life and saw Jesus. Just as the Holy Spirit had changed Spurgeon's heart in an instant at that quaint Primitive Methodist Chapel, so too the Spirit ushered Spurgeon into glory from the picturesque Hôtel Beau Rivage of southern France.

Spurgeon believed that every blessing in his life, from regeneration through final perseverance, was a direct result of the Holy Spirit's work in him. He celebrated the work of the Spirit in his own life, and proclaimed the great need of the Spirit in the life of every person. Truly, Spurgeon praised and adored "that blessed, blessed giver of all good, the Holy Ghost."[41]

---

38.   *MTP* 38.73.

39.   *MTP* 38.74.

40.   *MTP* 38.75.

41.   *MTP* 8.459.

W. Poole Balfern once described Spurgeon as being *"cradled in the Holy Ghost."*[42] Indeed, to borrow Balfern's phrase, Charles Haddon Spurgeon's life, theology, and ministry were cradled in the Holy Ghost.

42. *Autobiography* 2.192.

Works Cited

Primary Sources

Gregory of Nazianzus, *Oration 38: On the Theophany, or Birthday of Christ*. Edited by Philip Schaff and Henry Wace. *A Select Library of Nicene and Post-Nicene Fathers of the Christian Church*. 28 vols. Grand Rapids: Christian Classics Ethereal Library, 2016.

Hodge, Charles. *Systematic Theology*. 3 vols. New York: Scribner, Armstrong, and Co., 1873.

Karr, Alphonse. *A Tour Round My Garden*. Translated by J. G. Wood. London: G. Routledge, & Co., 1855.

Keach, Benjamin. *The Baptist Catechism: Commonly Called Keach's Catechism; or, a Brief Instruction in the Principles of the Christian Religion*. Philadelphia: American Baptist Publication Society, 1851.

Kuyper, Abraham. *The Work of the Holy Spirit*. Translated by Henri De Vries. New York: Funk & Wagnalls Company, 1900.

Milton, John. *Paradise Lost*. Edited by A. W. Verity. Cambridge: Cambridge University Press, 1910.

Owen, John. *The Works of John Owen*. Edited by William H. Goold. 37 vol. London: Johnstone and Hunter, 1850–1855.

Peabody, A. P. "Sermons of the Rev. C. H. Spurgeon, of London by C. H. Spurgeon; Fast-Day Service, Held at the Crystal Palace, Sydenham, on Wednesday, October 7th, 1857 by C. H. Spurgeon; The Saint and His Saviour, or the Progress of the Soul in the Knowledge of Jesus by C. H. Spurgeon." *The North American Review* 178 (January 1858): 275–80.

_____. "The Modern Whitefield: The Rev. C. H. Spurgeon, of London. His Sermons. With an Introduction and Sketch of His Life by E. L. Magoon." *The North American Review* 173 (October 1856): 553–54.

Pepperell, William. *The Church Index: A Book of Metropolitan Churches and Church Enterprise—Part I. Kensington.* London: W. Wells Gardner, 1872.

Spurgeon, Charles H. *An All-Round Ministry: Direction, Wisdom, and Encouragement for Preachers and Pastors.* Edinburgh: Banner of Truth Trust, 2018.

_____. *John Ploughman's Pictures.* Philadelphia: Henry Altemus, 1896.

_____. *The Letters of Charles Haddon Spurgeon: Collected and Collated by His Son.* Edited by Charles Spurgeon. London: Marshall Brothers, 1923.

_____. *The Lost Sermons of C. H. Spurgeon.* Vols. 1–7. Edited by Christian George, Jason Duesing, Geoffrey Chang, Phillip Ort. Nashville: B&H Academic, 2016–2022.

_____. *My Sermon Notes: A Selection from Outlines of Discourses Delivered at the Metropolitan Tabernacle.* Vols. 1–4. New York: Fleming H. Revell Company, 1884.

_____. *The Metropolitan Tabernacle Pulpit: Sermons Preached and Revised by C. H. Spurgeon.* Vols. 7–63. Pasadena, TX: Pilgrim Publications, 1970–2006.

_____. *The New Park Street Pulpit: Containing Sermons Preached and Revised by the Rev. C. H. Spurgeon, Minister of the Chapel.* Vols. 1– 6. Pasadena, TX: Pilgrim Publications, 1975–1991.

_____. *A Puritan Catechism with Proofs.* Albany, OR: Ages Digital Library, 1996.

_____. *The Suffering Letters of C H Spurgeon.* Edited by Hannah Wyncoll. London: Wakeman Trust, 2016.

_____. *The Sword and the Trowel; A Record of Combat with Sin & Labor for the Lord.* 37 Vols. London: Passmore & Alabaster, 1865–1902.

_____. *"Till He Come": Communion Meditations and Addresses.* London: Passmore & Alabaster, 1896.

_____. *The Treasury of David: Containing an Original Exposition of the Book of Psalms; A Collection of Illustrative Extracts from the Whole Range of Literature; A Series of Homiletical Hints Upon Almost Every Verse; And Lists of Writers Upon Each Psalm.* 7 Vols. London: Passmore & Alabaster, 1869–1885.

Spurgeon, Charles H., Susannah Spurgeon, and Joseph William Harrald, *Autobiography of Charles H. Spurgeon: Compiled from His Diary, Letters, and Records, by His Wife and His Private Secretary.* Vols. 1–4. Cincinnati: Curts & Jennings, 1898.

Stead, William Thomas. "Mr. Spurgeon at Home," *The Pall Mall Gazette*, June 18, 1884.

Witsius, Herman. *The Œconomy of the Covenants, between God and Man: Comprehending a Complete Body of Divinity.* New York: Thomas Kirk, 1798.

"Charles Spurgeon and the Pulpit." *Dublin Evening Packet and Correspondent*, August 1, 1857.

A Confession of Faith, Put forth by the Elders and Brethren of Many Congregations of Christians [Baptized upon Profession of their Faith in London and the Country (1689)]. Repr. in *The Philadelphia Confession of Faith; Being the London Confession of 1689,* 6th ed. Philadelphia: American Baptist Publication Society, 1907.

"The Death of the Rev. J. A. Spurgeon." *New Zealand Herald*, May 2, 1899.

"Mr. Spurgeon." *Salisbury and Winchester Journal*, June 15, 1861.

Thirty-Two Articles of Christian Faith and Practice; or, Baptist Confession of faith, with Scripture Proofs, Adopted by the Ministers and Messengers of the General Assembly, Which Met in London in 1689, with a Preface by the Rev. C. H. Spurgeon, 3rd ed. London: Passmore & Alabaster, 1857.

Wonders of Grace: Original Testimonies of Converts During Spurgeon's Early Years. Compiled by Hannah Wyncoll. London: The Wakeman Trust, 2016.

Secondary Sources

Bacon, Ernest W. *Spurgeon: Heir of the Puritans*. Grand Rapids: Eerdmans Publishing Company, 1968.

Brown, Francis, S. R. Driver, and C. A. Briggs. *The Brown-Driver-Briggs Hebrew and English Lexicon*. Peabody: Hendrickson Publishers, 1981.

Chang, Geoffrey. *The Army of God: Spurgeon's Vision for the Church*. Ross-shire, Scotland: Christian Focus Publications, 2024.

_____. *Spurgeon the Pastor: Recovering a Biblical & Theological Vision for Ministry*. Nashville: B&H Publishing, 2022.

Chang, Geoffrey and Alex DiPrima, eds. *Spurgeon in Context: History, Theology, and Ministry*. Brentwood: B&H Publishing Group, 2025.

Carneiro, Ilona and Natasha Howard. *Introduction to Epidemiology*, 2nd edition. Maidenhead: Open University Press, 2011.

Fullerton, W. Y. *C. H. Spurgeon: A Biography*. London: Williams and Norgate, 1920.

Haykin, Michael A. G. "'Where the Spirit of God Is, There Is Power': An Introduction to Spurgeon's Teaching on the Holy Spirit." *Churchman* 3 (1992): 197–208.

Kittel, Gerhard and Gerhard Friedrich, eds. *Theological Dictionary of the New Testament*, 10 vols. Grand Rapids: Eerdmans, 1964–1976.

Lumpkin, William L. *Baptist Confessions of Faith*. Valley Forge, PA: Judson, 1969.

Morden, Peter J. *Communion with Christ and His People: The Spirituality of C. H. Spurgeon*. Eugene, OR: Pickwick Publications, 2014.

Murray, Iain H. *The Forgotten Spurgeon*. Edinburgh: Banner of Truth Trust, 2009.

Nettles, Tom J. *Living by Revealed Truth: The Life and Pastoral Theology of Charles Haddon Spurgeon.* Ross-shire, Scotland: Christian Focus Publications, 2015.

Nicholls, Michael. "Charles Haddon Spurgeon, Educationalist: Part 1 – General Educational Concerns." *Baptist Quarterly* 31, no. 8 (October 1986): 384–401.

_____. "Charles Haddon Spurgeon, Educationalist: Part 2, The Principles and Practice of Pastors' College." *Baptist Quarterly* 31, no. 2 (April 1887): 73–94.

Nuttall, Geoffrey F. *The Holy Spirit in Puritan Faith and Experience.* Oxford: Basil Blackwell, 1946.

Packer, J. I., ed. *Puritan Papers.* 5 vols. Phillipsburg, NJ: P & R Pub, 2000.

Thomas, Amanda J. *Cholera: The Victorian Plague.* Barnsley: Pen & Sword History, 2015.

Williams, William. *Personal Reminiscences of Charles Haddon Spurgeon.* London: The Religious Tract Society, 1895.

Index

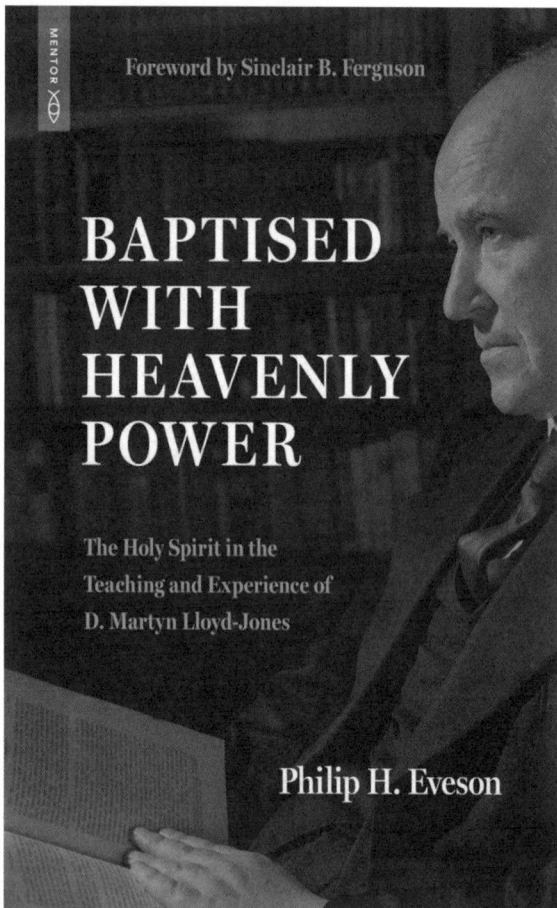

MENTOR

Foreword by Sinclair B. Ferguson

BAPTISED WITH HEAVENLY POWER

The Holy Spirit in the
Teaching and Experience of
D. Martyn Lloyd-Jones

Philip H. Eveson

Baptised with Heavenly Power
by Philip H. Eveson

This groundbreaking study examines D. Martyn Lloyd–Jones's theology of the Holy Spirit, particularly focusing on his controversial teaching about the baptism of the Spirit, revival, and the relationship between Word and Spirit in preaching. Drawing extensively on Lloyd–Jones's sermons, lectures, and previously unpublished materials, Philip Eveson demonstrates that Lloyd–Jones stood firmly within the Reformed tradition while emphasising the experiential aspect of Christianity that characterised early Calvinistic Methodism.

The book provides fresh insights into Lloyd–Jones's thinking by exploring his medical background, his Welsh Methodist roots, and his profound engagement with Puritan writers. It carefully analyses his understanding of Spirit baptism, assurance, and revival, showing how his position differed from both Pentecostalism and cessationism.

Particularly valuable is the detailed examination of Lloyd–Jones's philosophy of preaching and his insistence on both doctrinal accuracy and spiritual power. The author convincingly argues that Lloyd–Jones's emphasis on the Holy Spirit's work offers vital insights for contemporary Reformed Christianity.

Two valuable appendices provide previously unpublished material: Lloyd–Jones's important address on the Welsh Revival of 1904–05, and his personal spiritual journal from 1930–31. An extensive bibliography guides readers to primary and secondary sources for further study.

Essential reading for ministers, theological students, and anyone interested in Lloyd–Jones's legacy or the role of the Holy Spirit in Christian life and ministry.

ISBN: 978-1-5271-1253-7

Living by Revealed Truth
The Life and Pastoral Theology of Charles Haddon Spurgeon
by Tom Nettles

Tom Nettles has spent more than 15 years working on this magis-terial biography of Charles Haddon Spurgeon, the famous 19th century preacher and writer. More than merely a biography it covers his life, ministry and also provides an indepth survey of his theology.

... an "all-round" study of Spurgeon that provides us with a fully reliable, substantial examination of an extremely important figure in the life of Victorian Evangelicalism and the world of that era.

Michael A. G. Haykin
Professor of Church History and Biblical Spirituality,
The Southern Baptist Theological Seminary, Louisville, Kentucky.

ISBN: 978-1-78191-122-8

Spurgeon's Vision
for the Church

THE ARMY
OF GOD

Geoffrey Chang

SERIES EDITOR: GEOFFREY CHANG

The Army of God
Spurgeon's Vision for the Church
by Geoffrey Change

The figures associated with Charles Haddon Spurgeon's ministry are staggering. Between his preaching and the printings of his sermons, he reached hundreds of thousands of people, in his lifetime and in the years since. But he was not an itinerant preacher or writer or philanthropist. He faithfully served the Metropolitan Tabernacle from his arrival in 1854 to his death in 1892. Undergirding everything else was this central responsibility: Spurgeon was the pastor of a church.

What was Spurgeon's ecclesiology and how did it affect how he ordered and led his local church? Chang examines Spurgeon's Reformed ecclesiology and Baptist polity and looks at how they were shaped by his militant church outlook in this first book in the Spurgeon's Legacy series.

ISBN: 978-1-5271-0873-8

Christian Focus Publications

Our mission statement
Staying Faithful

In dependence upon God we seek to impact the world through literature faithful to His infallible Word, the Bible. Our aim is to ensure that the Lord Jesus Christ is presented as the only hope to obtain forgiveness of sin, live a useful life and look forward to heaven with Him.

Our Books are published in four imprints:

◁◁⋉ CHRISTIAN FOCUS

Popular works including biographies, commentaries, basic doctrine and Christian living.

◁◁⋉ MENTOR

Books written at a level suitable for Bible College and seminary students, pastors, and other serious readers. The imprint includes commentaries, doctrinal studies, examination of current issues and church history.

◁◁⋉ CHRISTIAN HERITAGE

Books representing some of the best material from the rich heritage of the church.

◁◁⋉ CF4KIDS

Children's books for quality Bible teaching and for all age groups: Sunday school curriculum, puzzle and activity books; personal and family devotional titles, biographies and inspirational stories – because you are never too young to know Jesus!

Christian Focus Publications Ltd,
Geanies House, Fearn, Ross-shire,
IV20 1TW, Scotland, United Kingdom.
www.christianfocus.com